THE *INSTAGLITCH* PROJECT

Michael Betancourt is a critical theorist and research artist who has cultivated a hybrid practice addressing media history, digital technology, and capitalist ideology. Author of more than thirty books, his deeply interdisciplinary writing has been translated into Chinese, French, German, Greek, Italian, Japanese, Persian, Portuguese, and Spanish. His critical analysis provides a model and foundation for his studio work. This analysis considers the contemporary global financialization of digital capitalism via the social and cultural impacts of AI, Bitcoin, surveillance, and Universal Basic Income (inter alia) as reflections of structural demands implicit in how the Enlightenment project informs both historical industrial capitalism and contemporary digital technology. He is a board member of the *Art of Light Organization.*

A pioneer of "Glitch Art," he has engaged the links between theory and practice by databending images and video since the 1990s. His visually seductive glitch works bring the visionary tradition into the present. By emphasizing their digital origins, his aesthetics encourages the viewer to find poetic meaning in their everyday life. His movies and statics have shown internationally at film festivals and art fairs, including the *Black Maria Film Festival, Art Basel Miami Beach, Contemporary Art Ruhr, Athens Video Art Festival, Festival des Cinemas Differents de Paris, Anthology Film Archives, Millennium Film Workshop,* the San Francisco Cinematheque's *Crossroads,* and *Experiments in Cinema,* among others. One of his games-as-art, *Toonzy! The Cartoon Role-Playing Game,* was nominated for an Ennie Award as Best Free Game in 2016. His interactive publication the ____________ *Manifesto* is a well known work of interactive net.art from the 1990s. This aesthetic work is informed by ground breaking historical research: in 2006, he found the oldest surviving hand-painted abstract films (produced in 1916 by Mary Hallock-Greenewalt). He also wrote the first history of motion graphics in the United States charting its origins to the commercial appropriation of avant-garde film and video art.

His archive is located at *michaelbetancourt.com*

THE *INSTAGLITCH* PROJECT

MICHAEL BETANCOURT

a selection from 2,600 Instaglitches

2016 — 2021

I'M PRESS'D
SAVANNAH\GEORGIA

Published by I'M PRESS'D
an imprint of Cinegraphic Media

for Leah

www.michaelbetancourt.com

interior: originally posed to *@glitcharts*, 2016 – 2021

ISBN 978-0-9793215-2-8

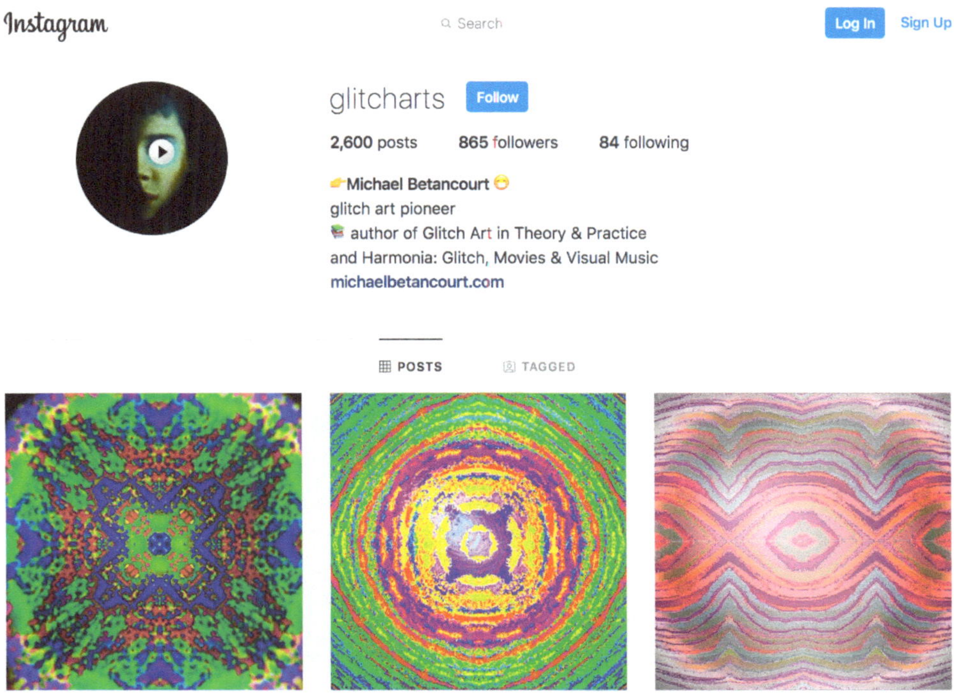

Michael Betancourt's "*Instaglitch* Project" exploits the aberrant and *unheimlich* results of image handling and processing by the *Instagram* photosharing app to derive novel examples of Glitch Art from the faults inherent to the *iPhone* system. This project uses these inconsistencies as a mechanism for aesthetic creation that provides evidence for the fantasy of control that the "walled garden" of apps create. The development of the *Instaglitch* offers a counter to this hegemonic ideology via a studio practice that exploits the *Instagram* app's very limited 'degrees of freedom' without altering the app itself or employing less restrictive software. These works are examples of how repeated processing and 'filtering' of the same image within the same system—a feedback loop—magnifies the instabilities inherent in its operations. The 2,600 works in this series of static images demonstrates programmatic failures that are masked by the normal, vernacular use of *Instagram,* but which are systemic instabilities—their identification allowed the generation of works by manipulating their impacts on a blank (white) image.

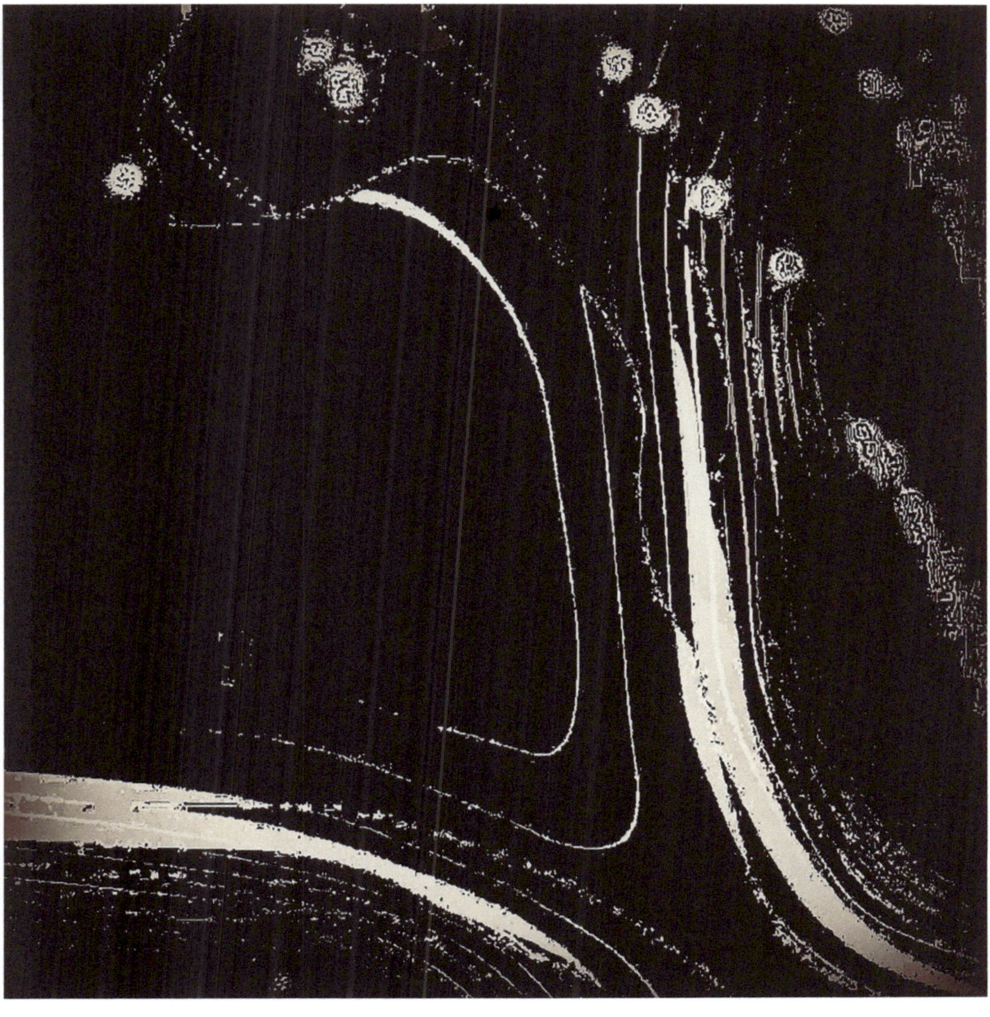

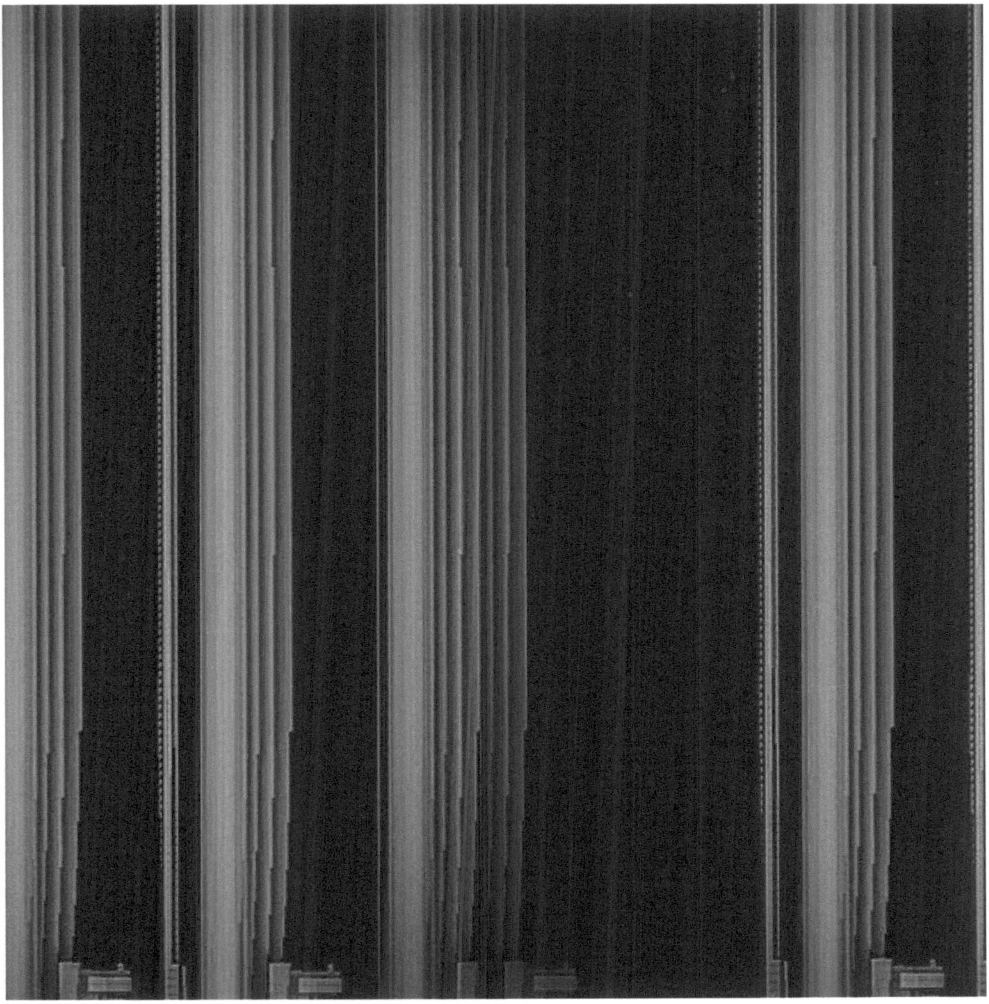

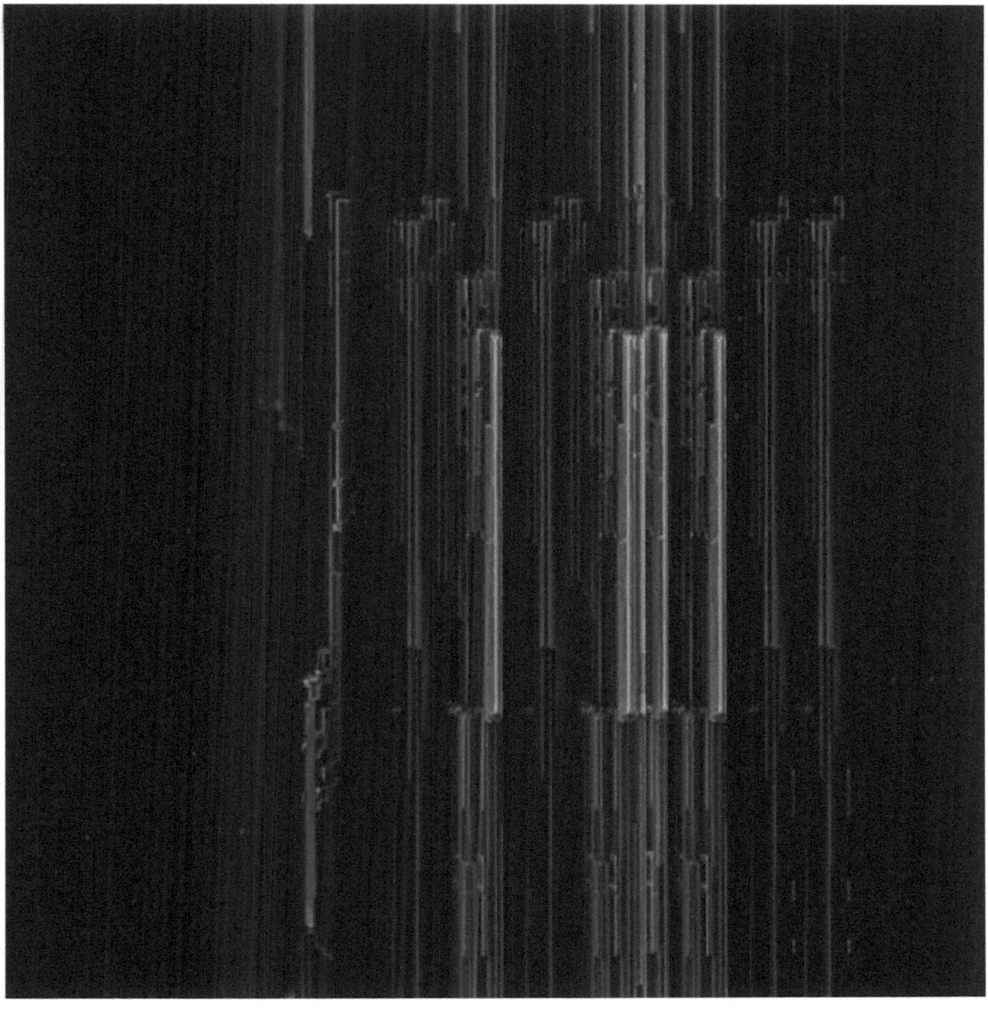

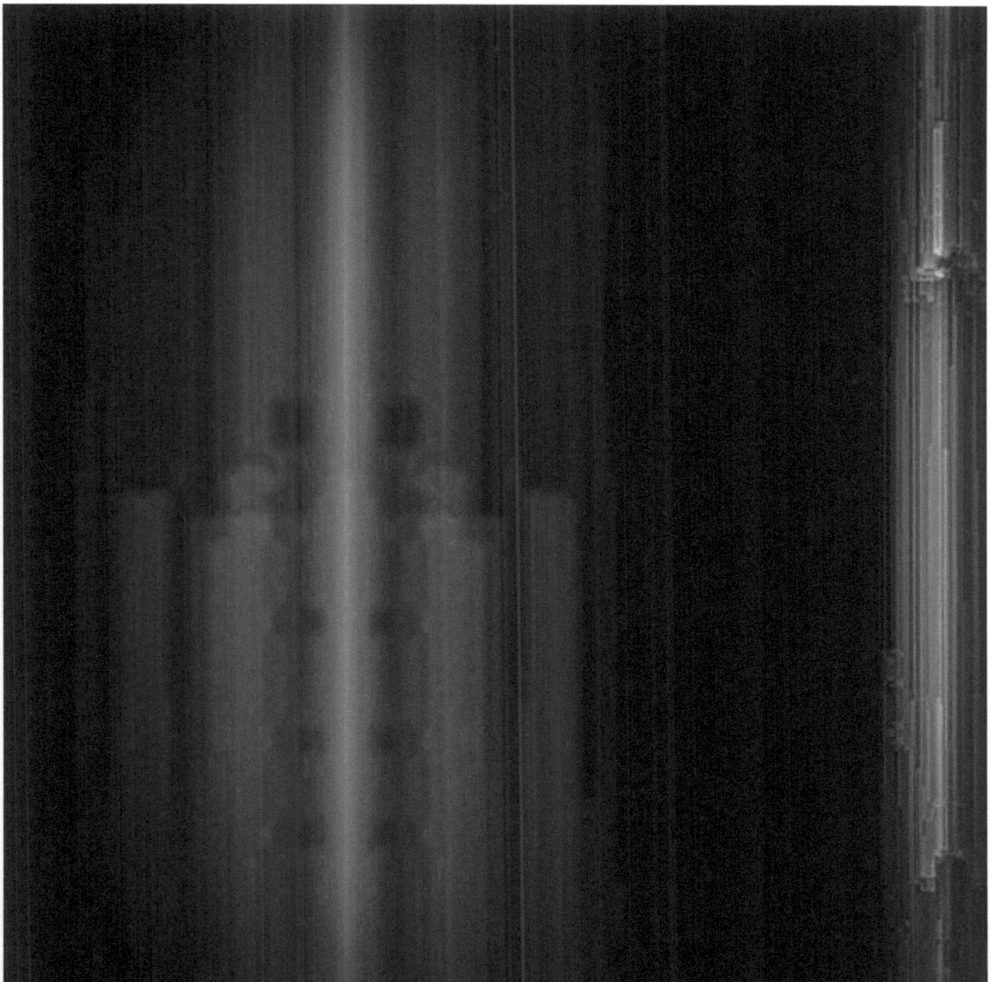

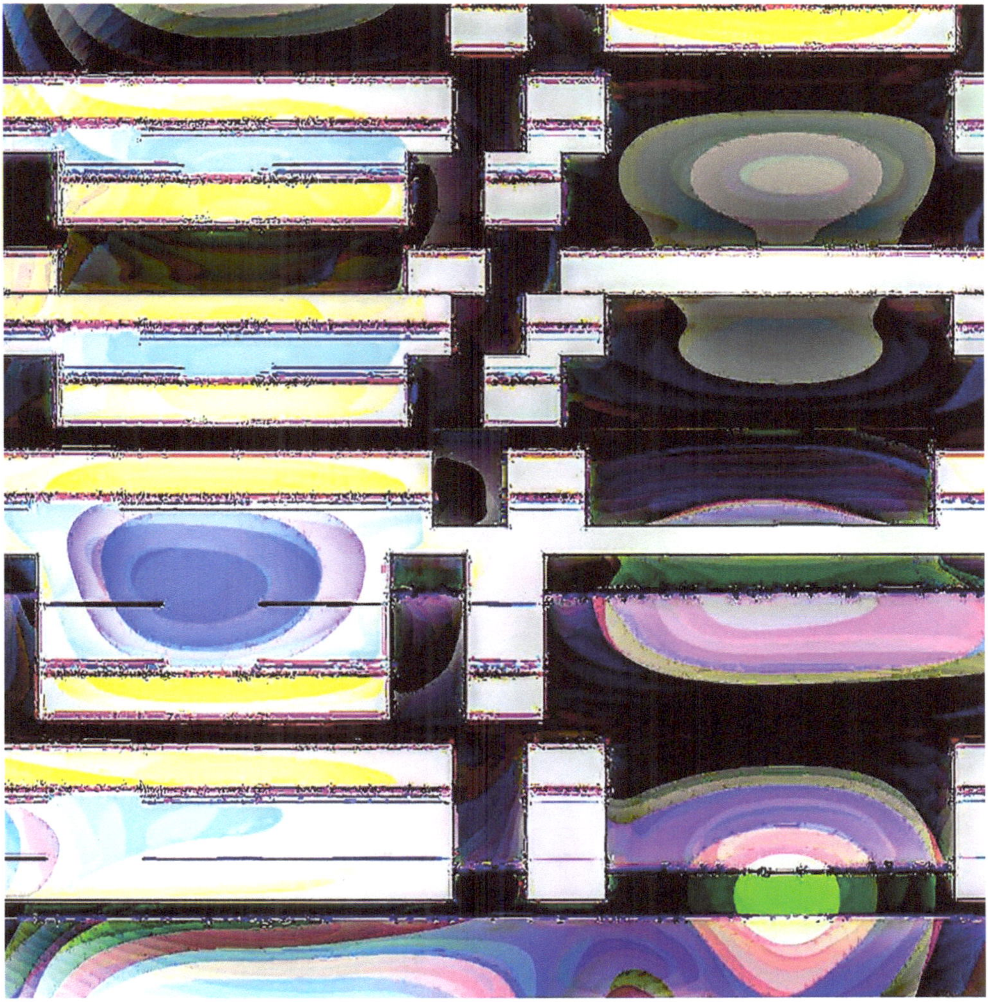

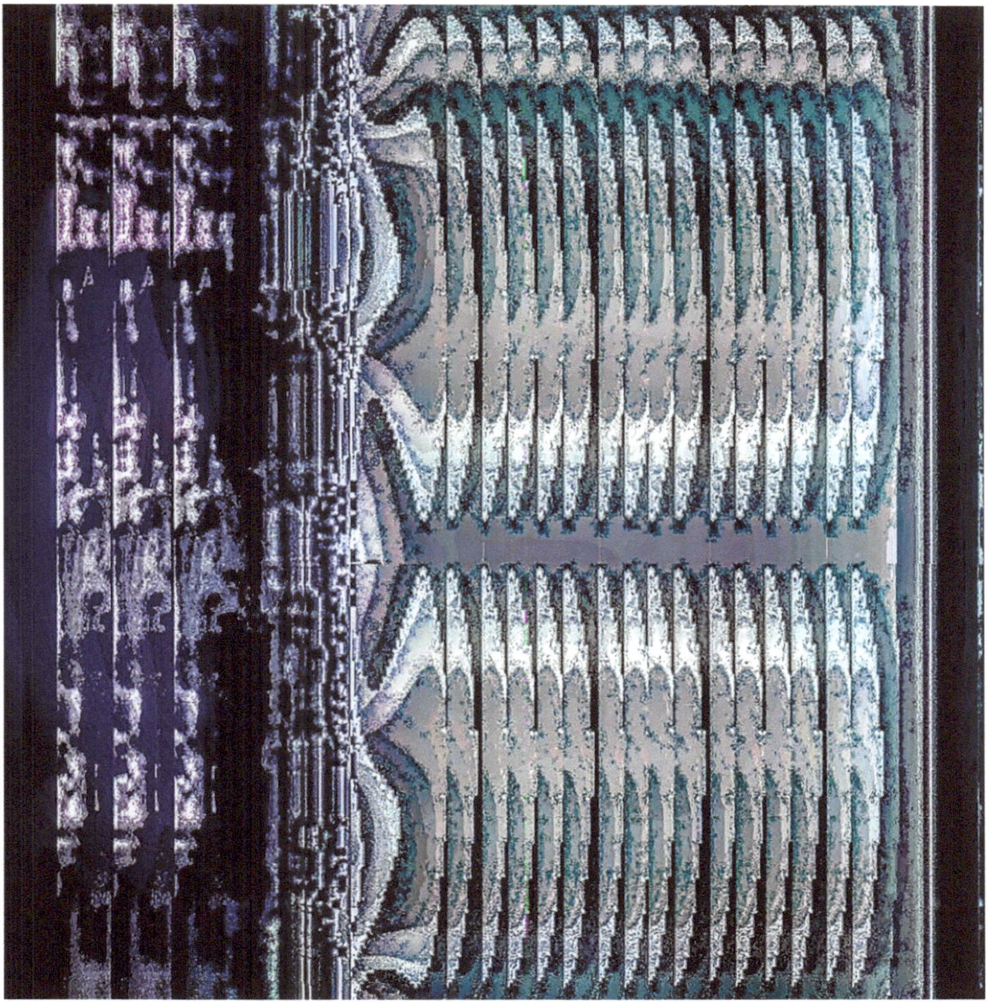

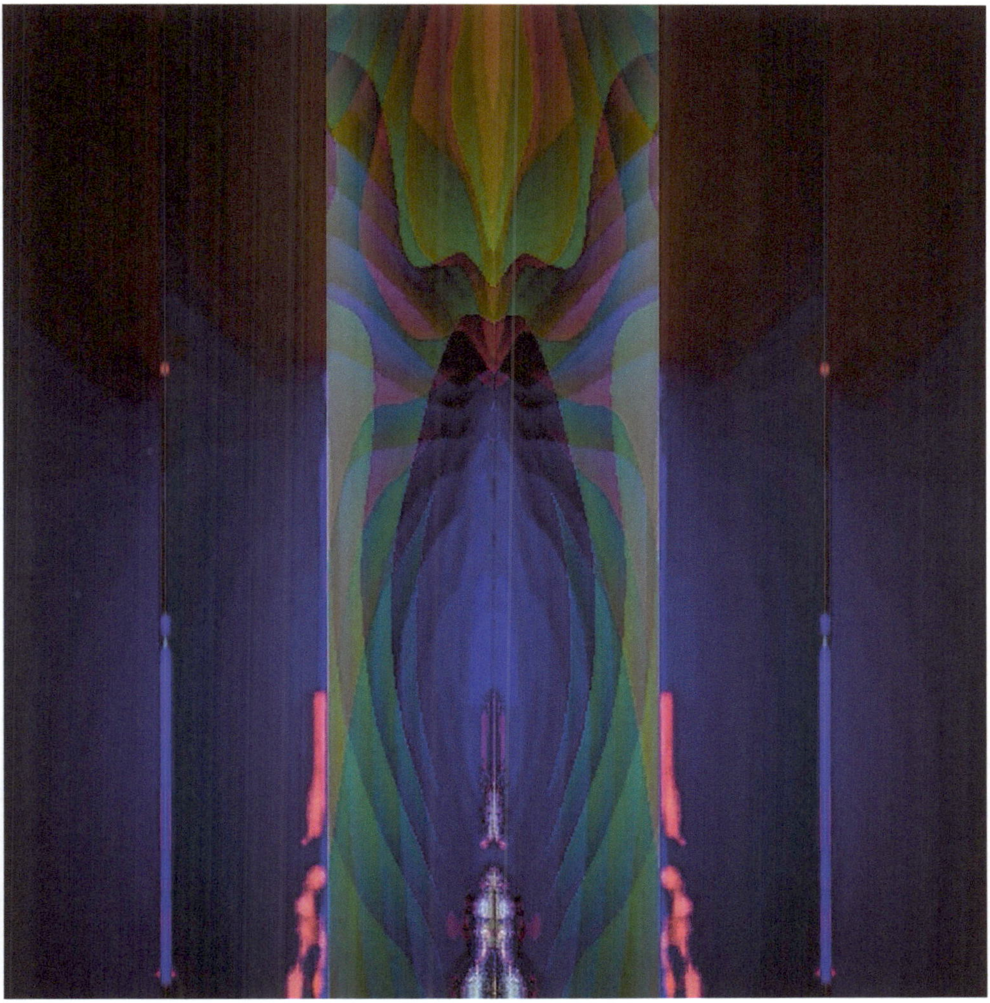

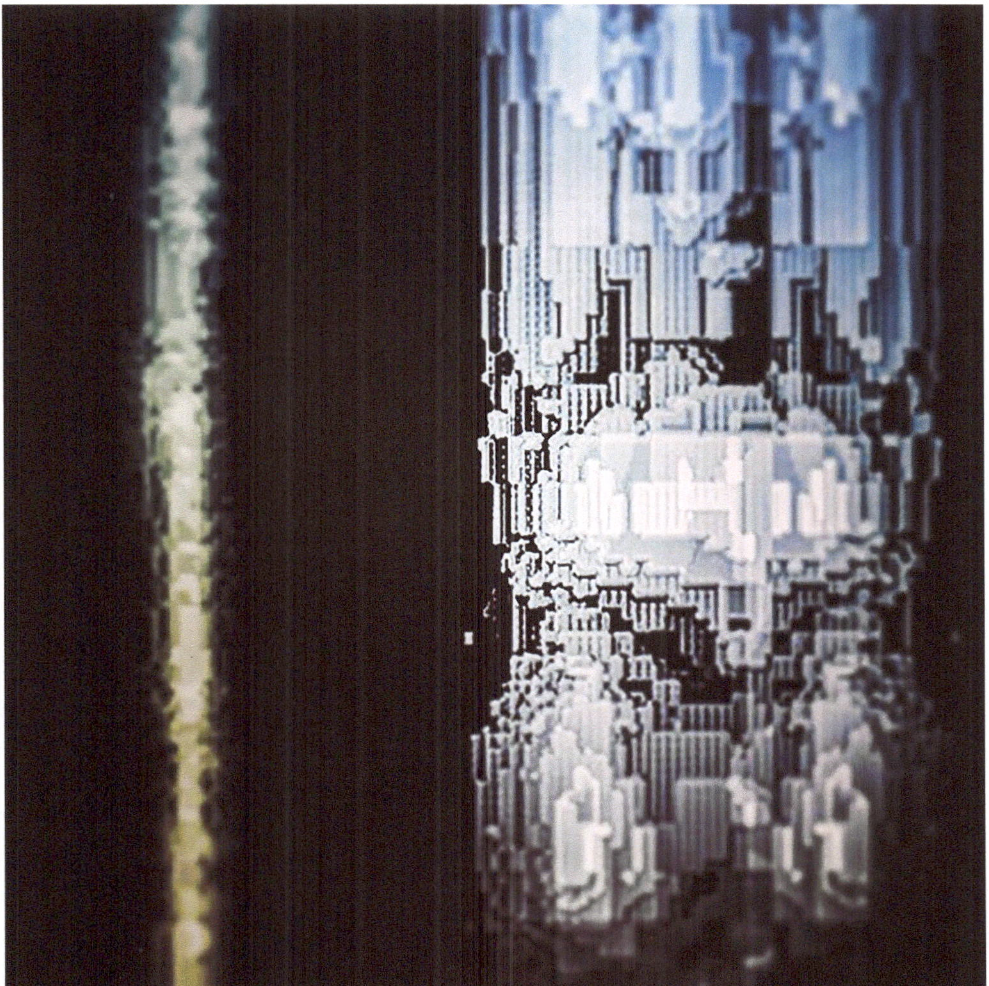

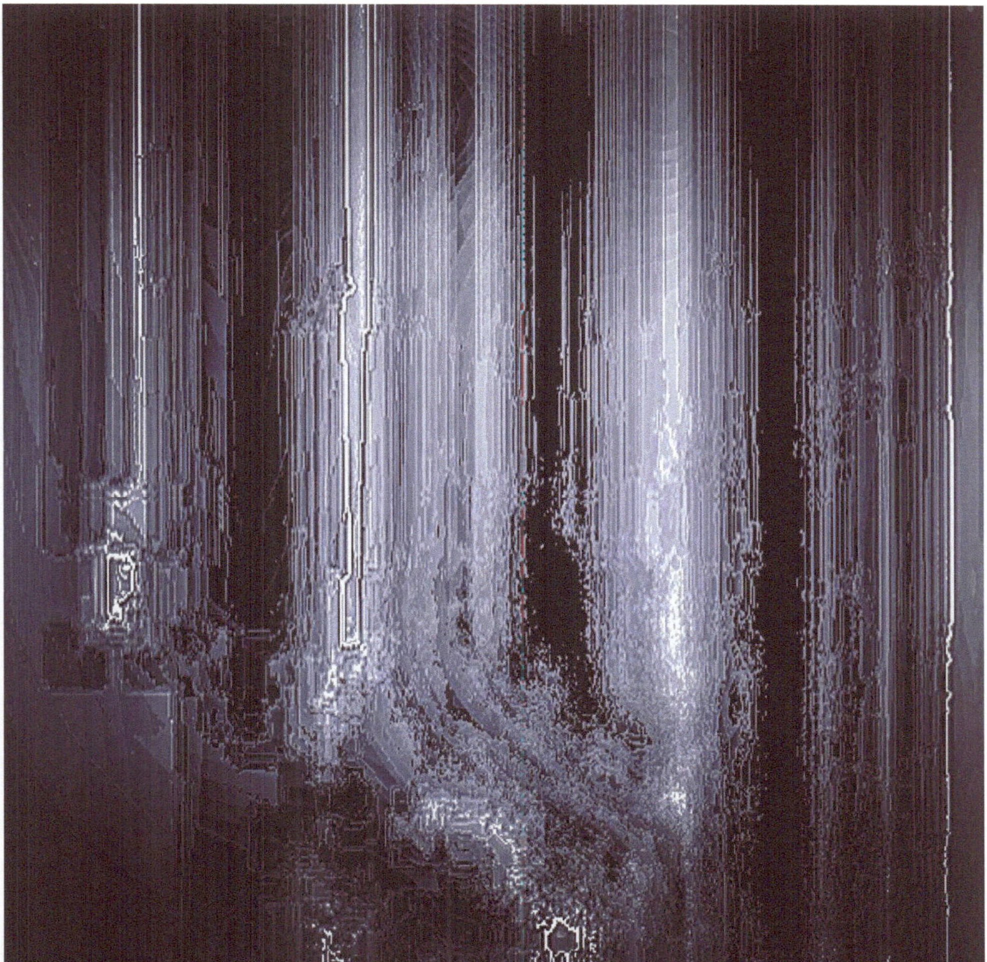

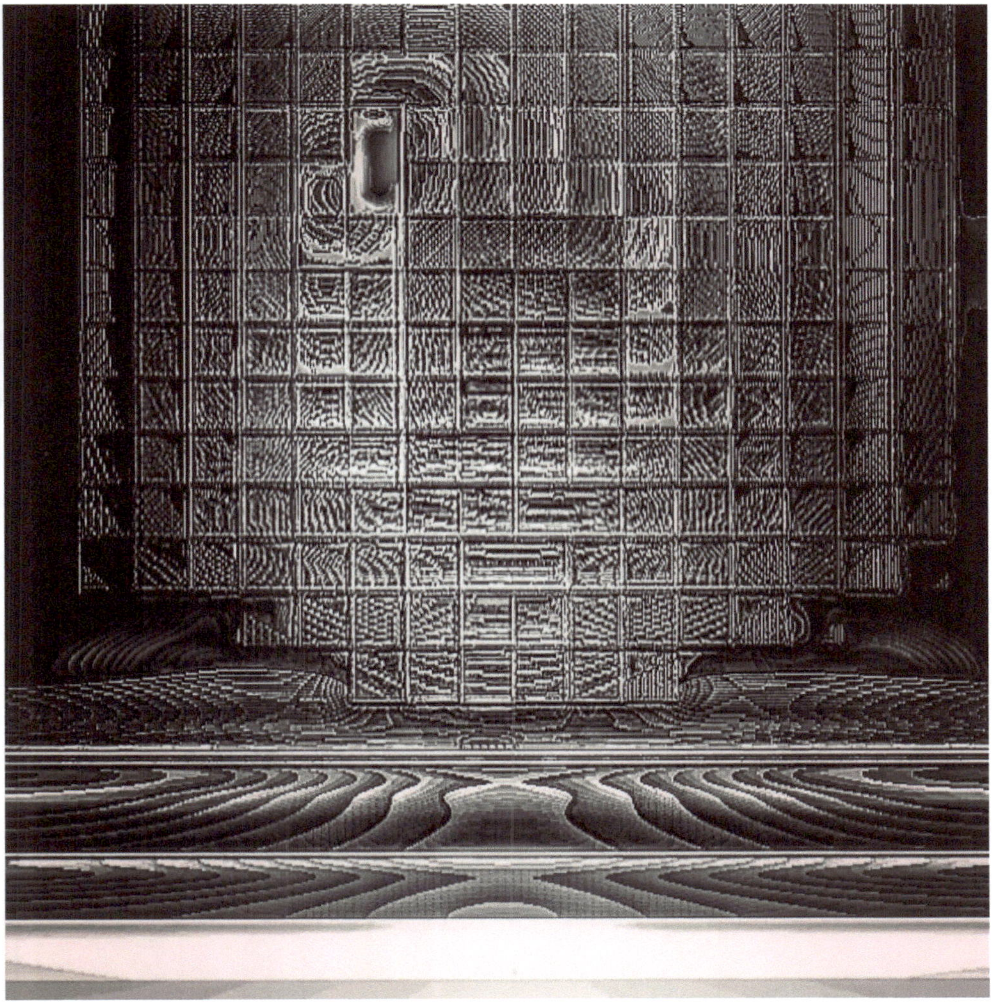

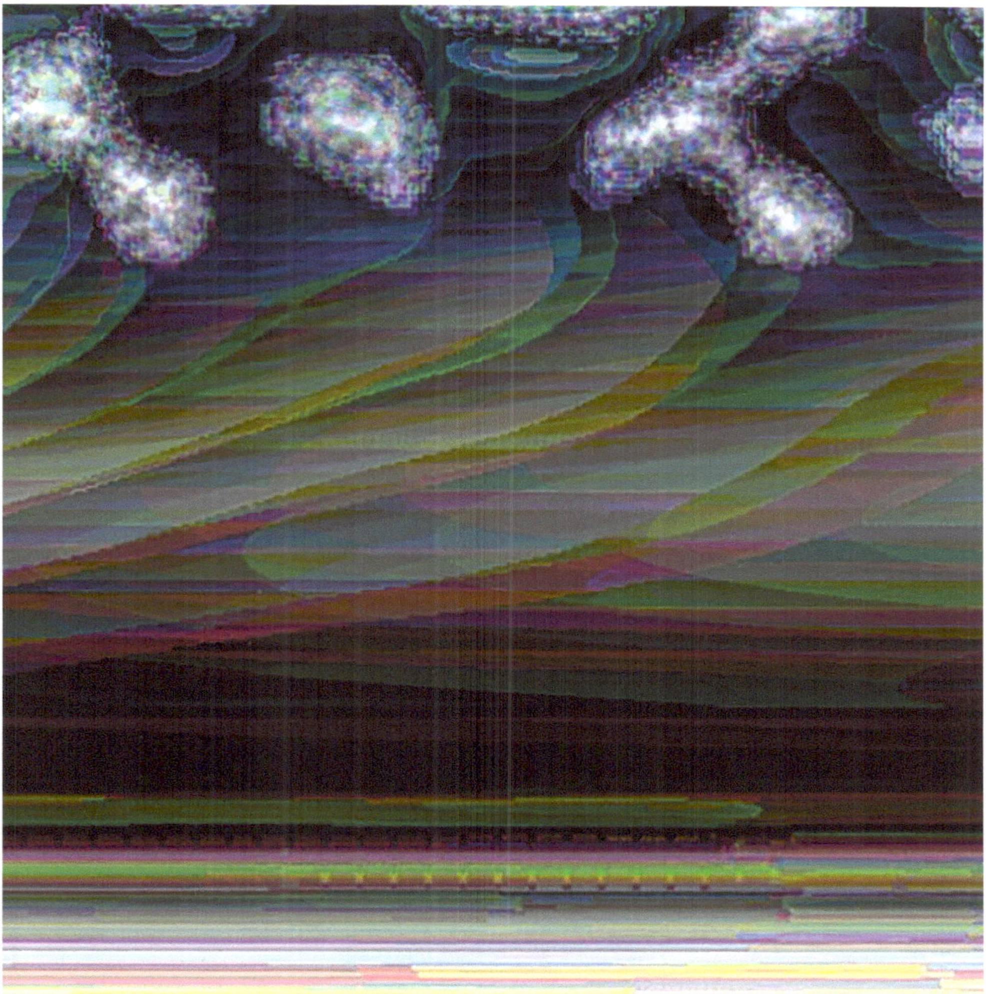

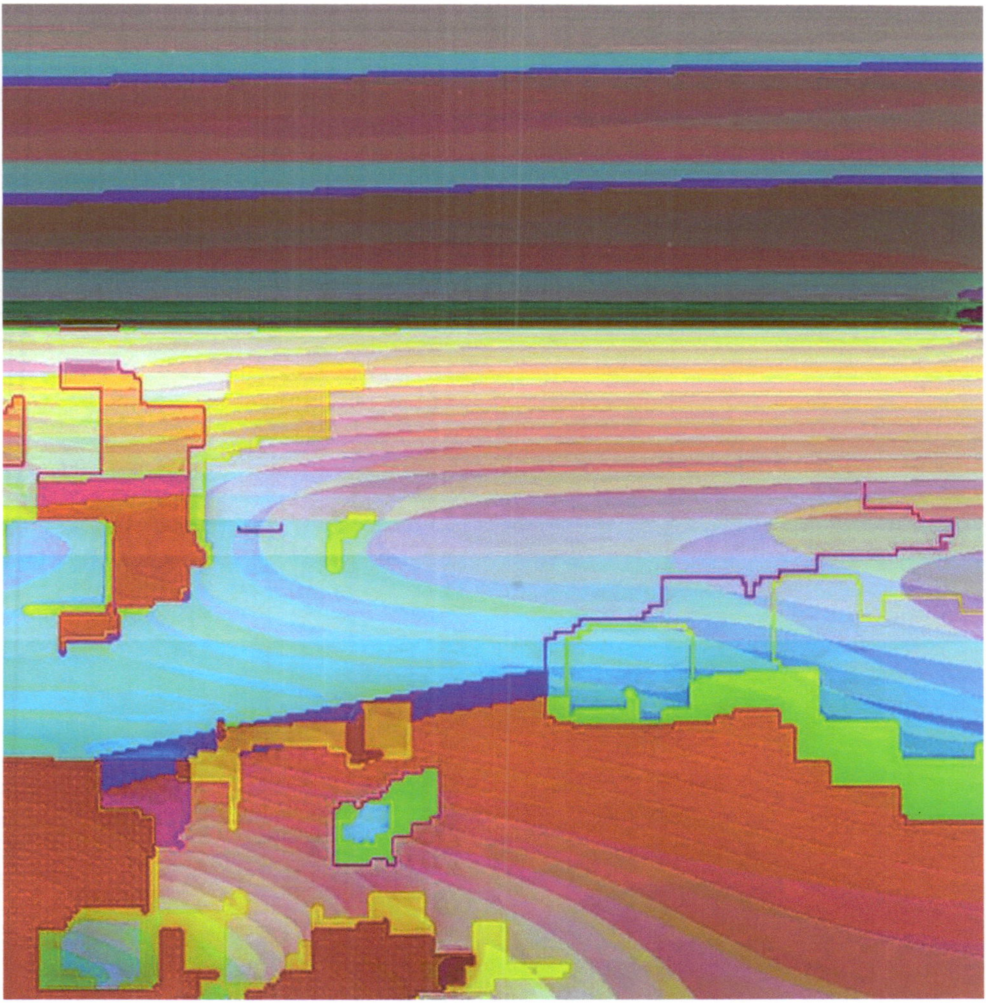

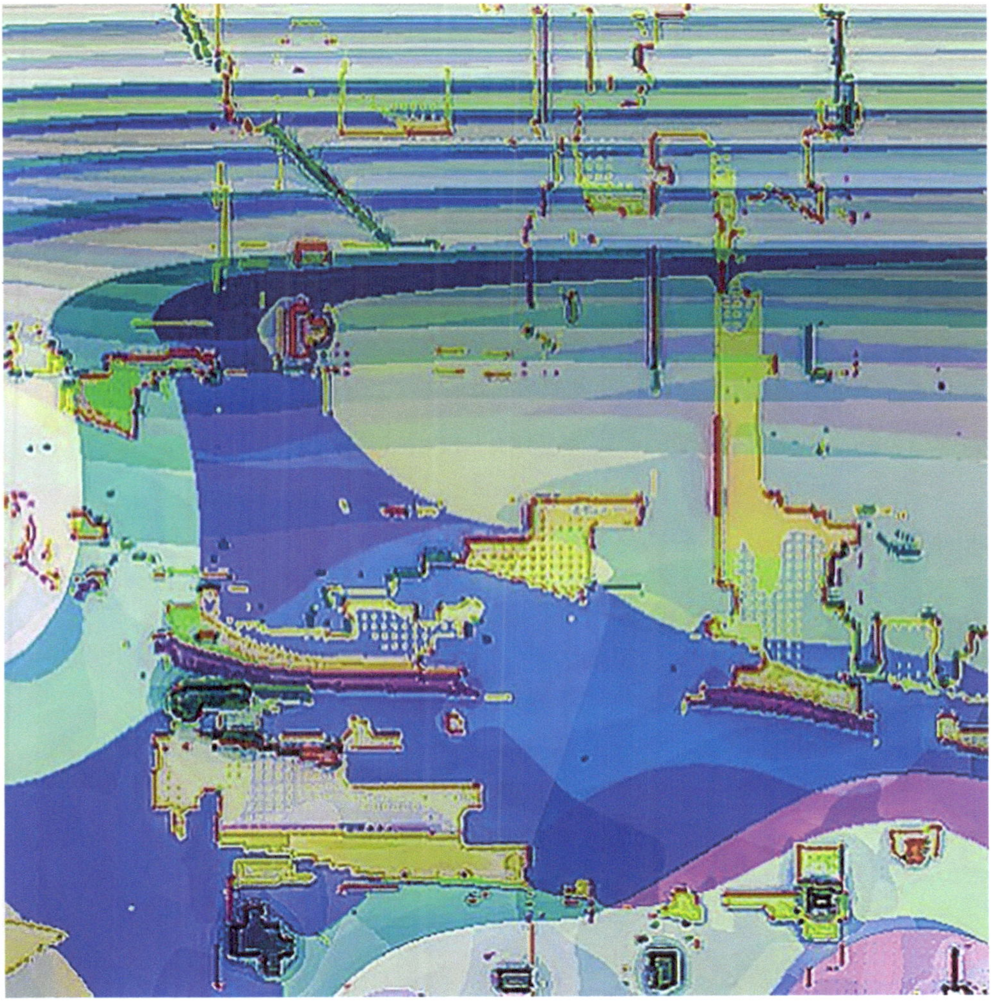

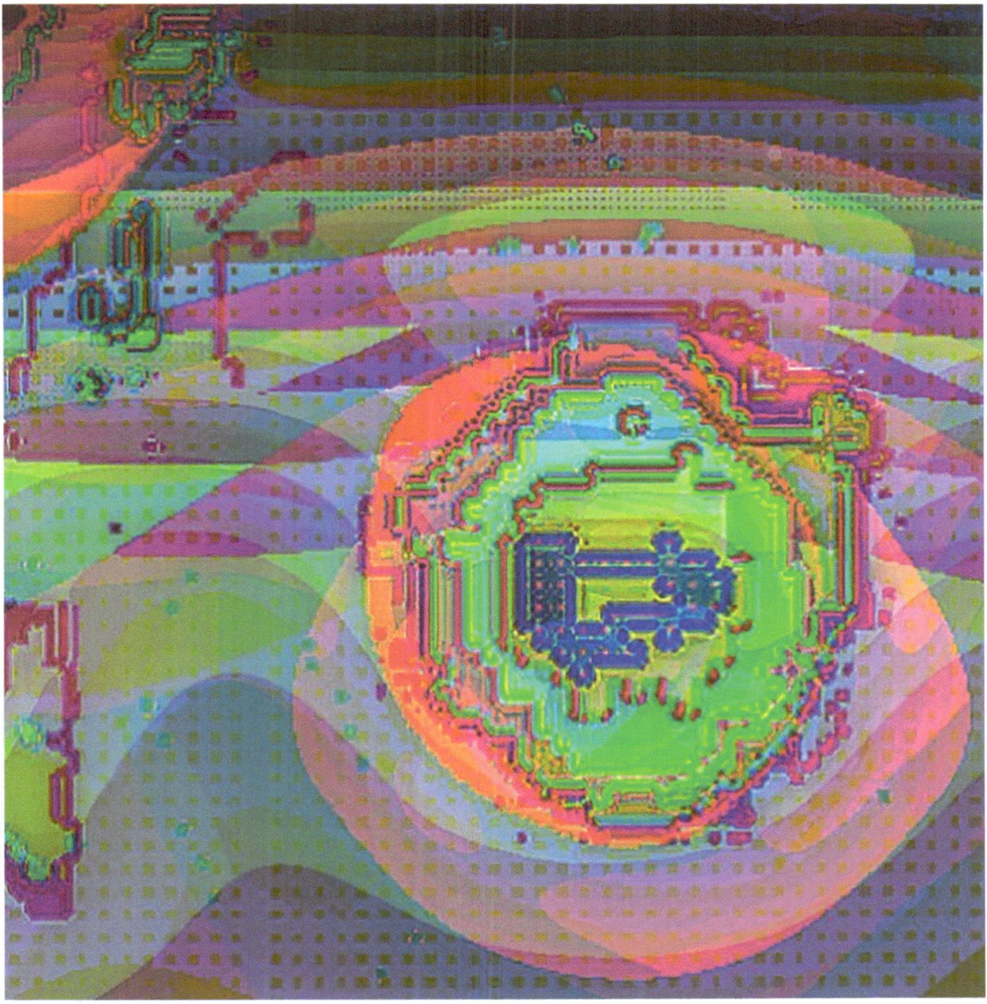

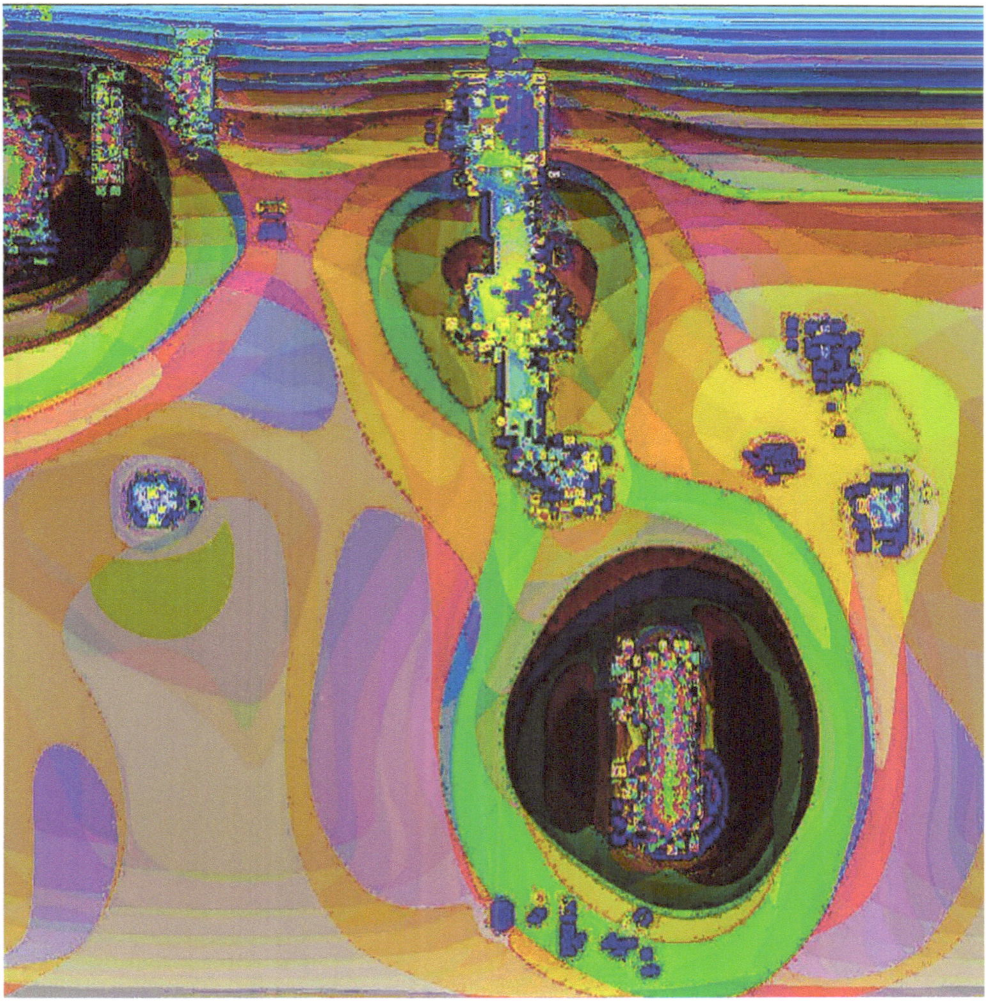

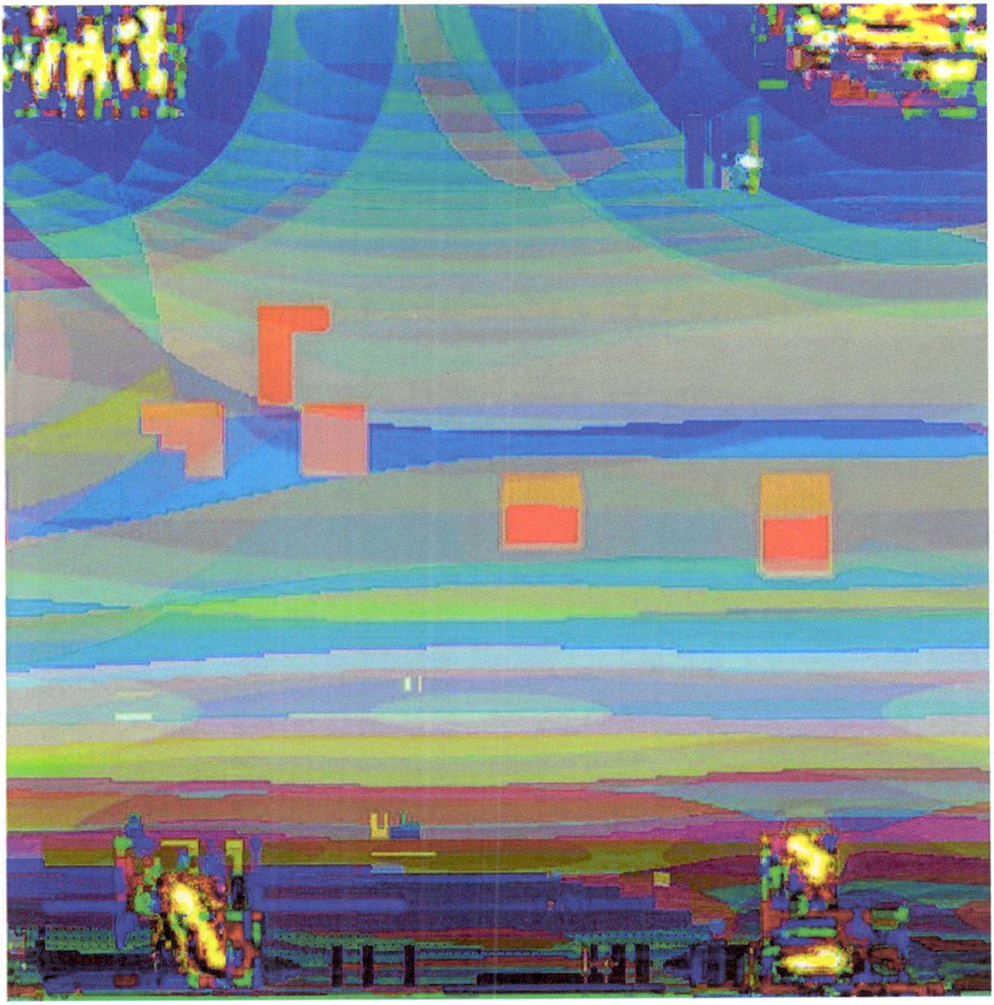

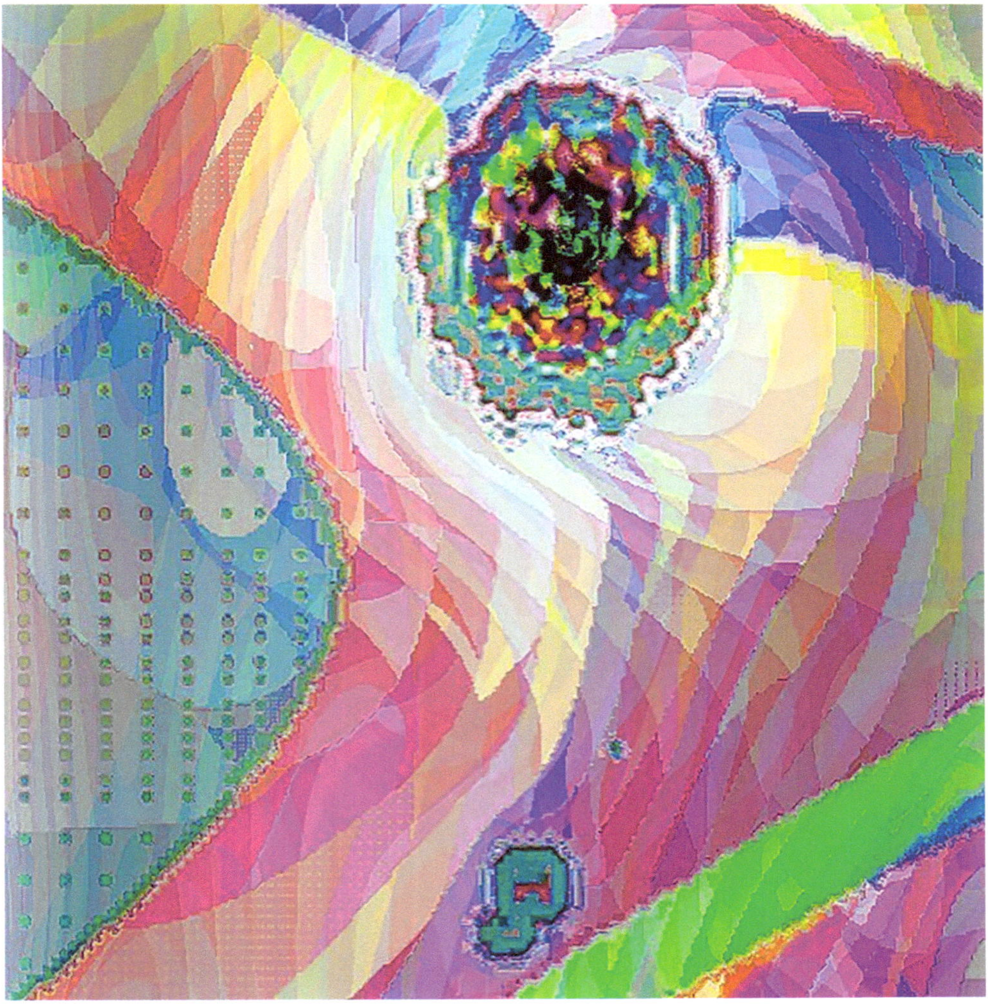

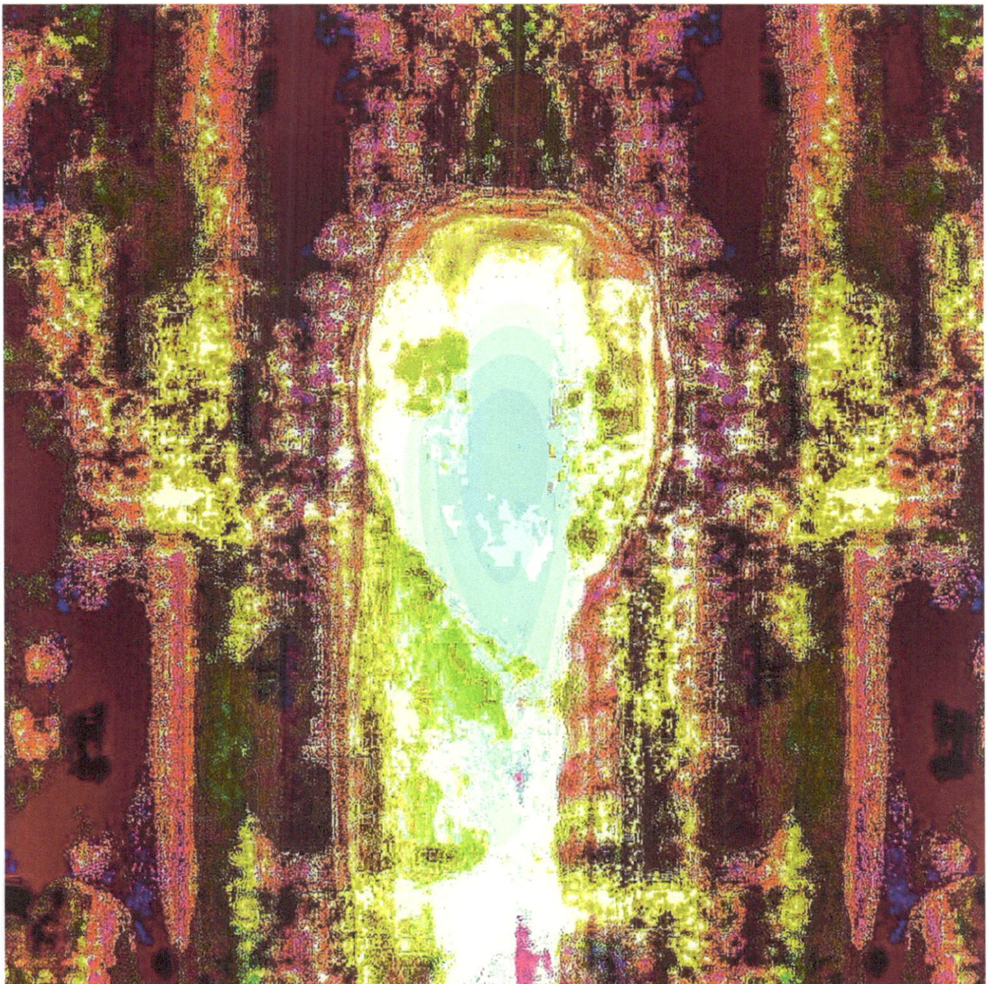

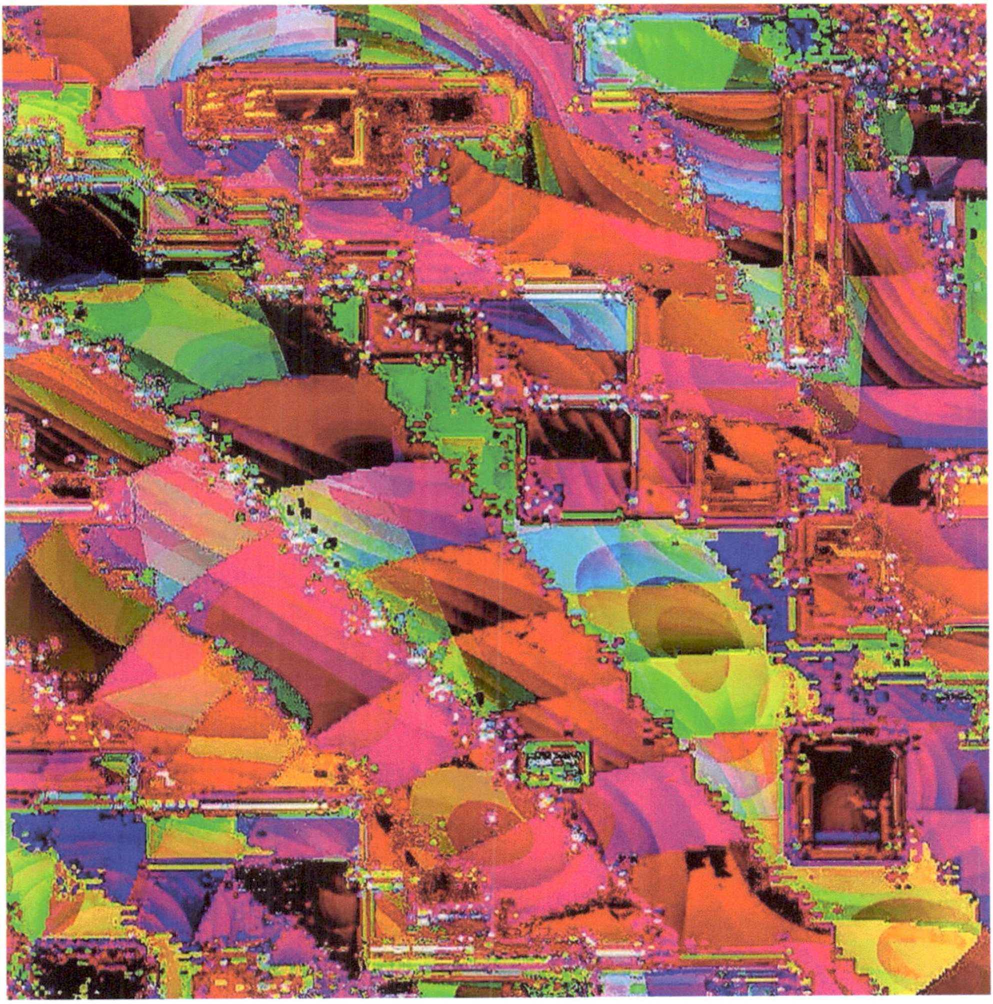

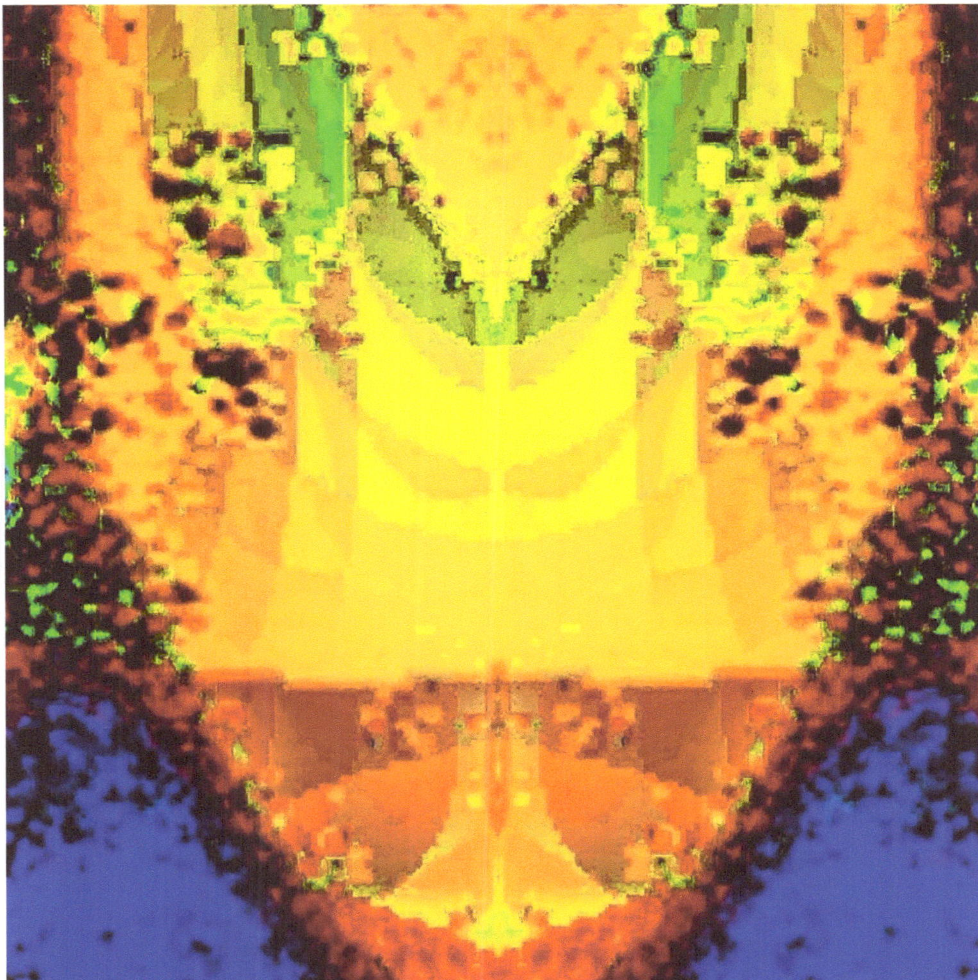

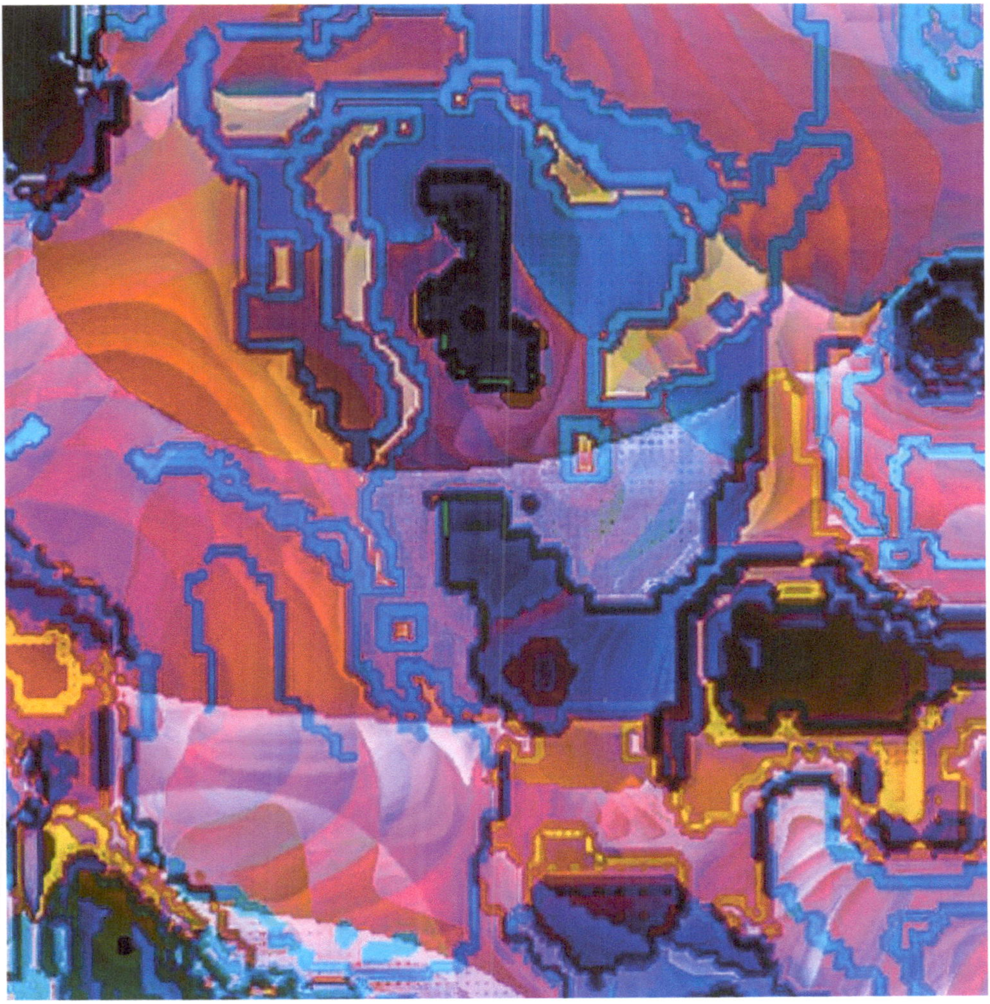

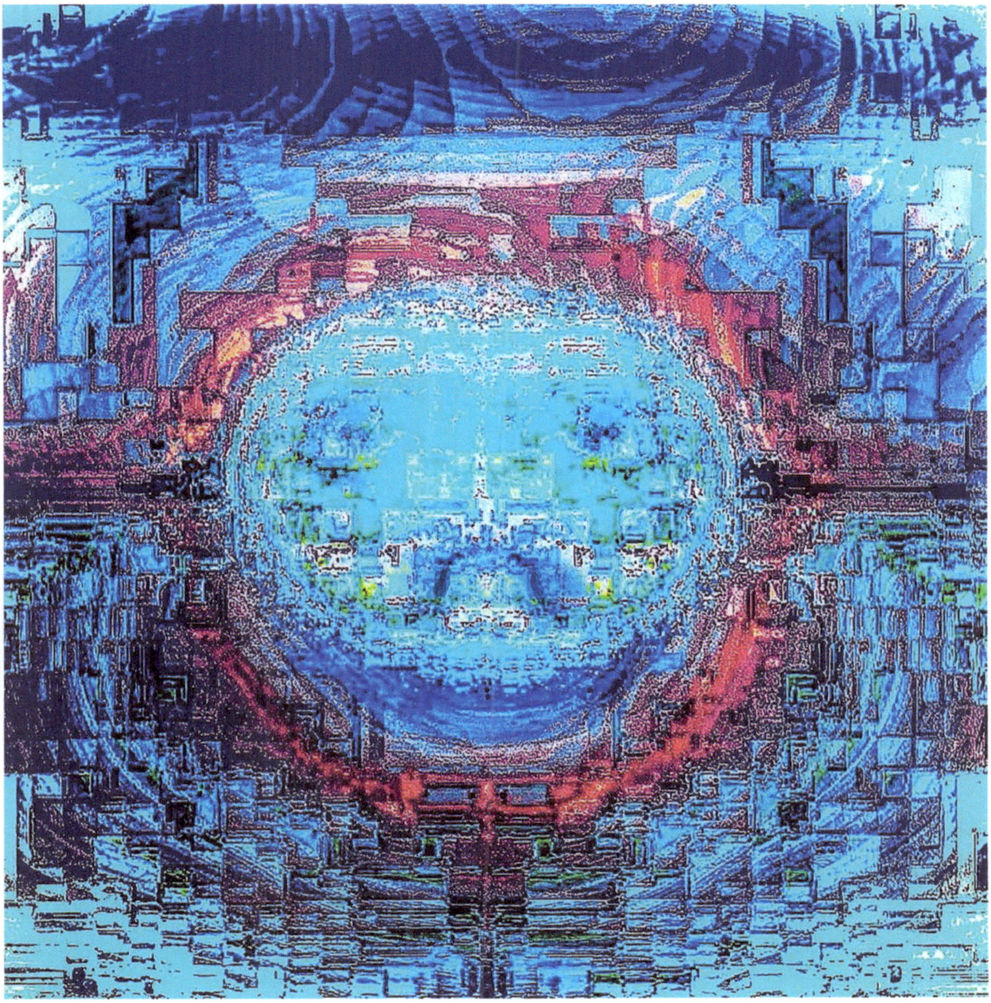

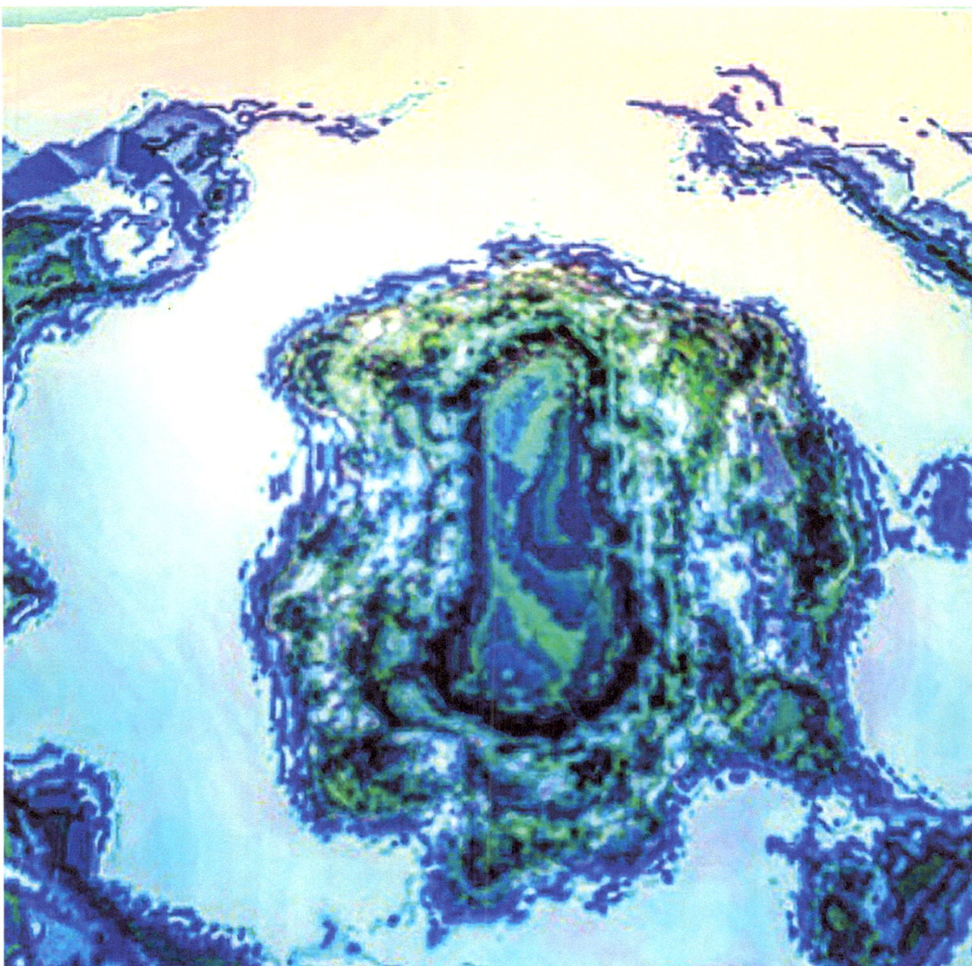

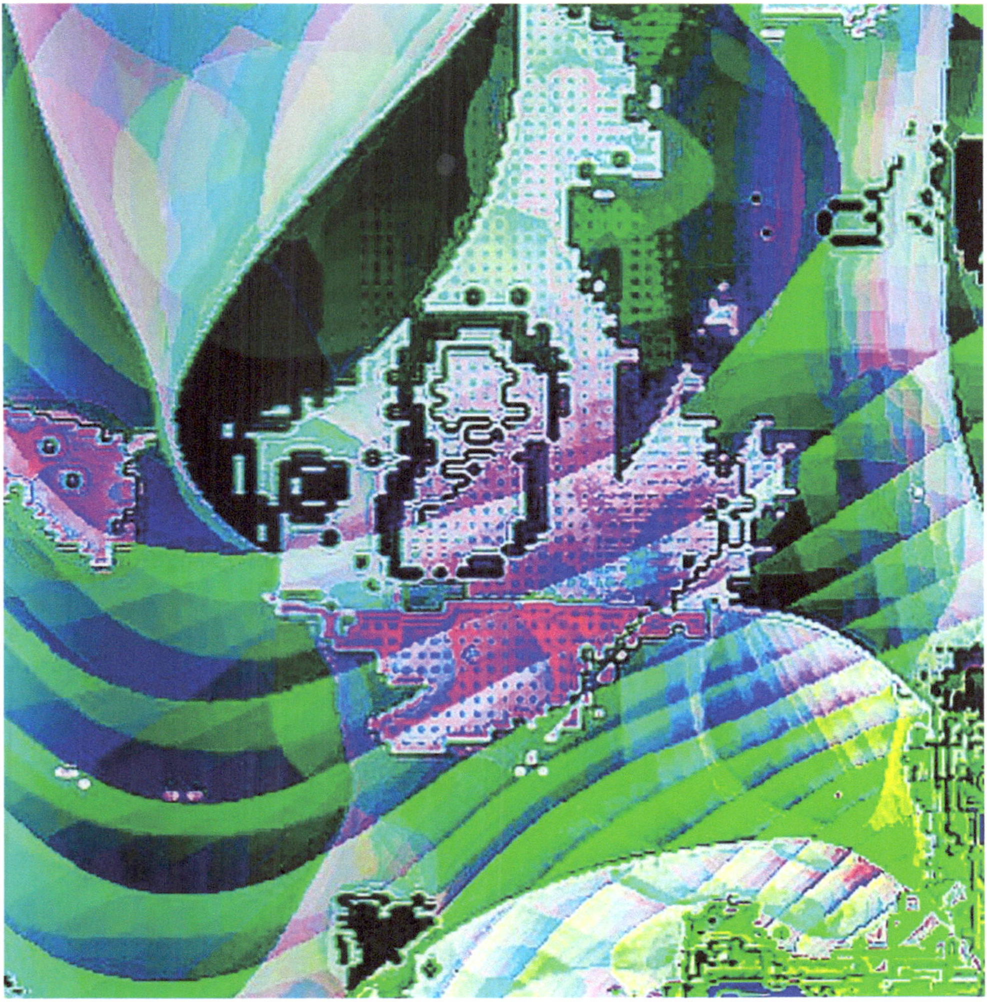

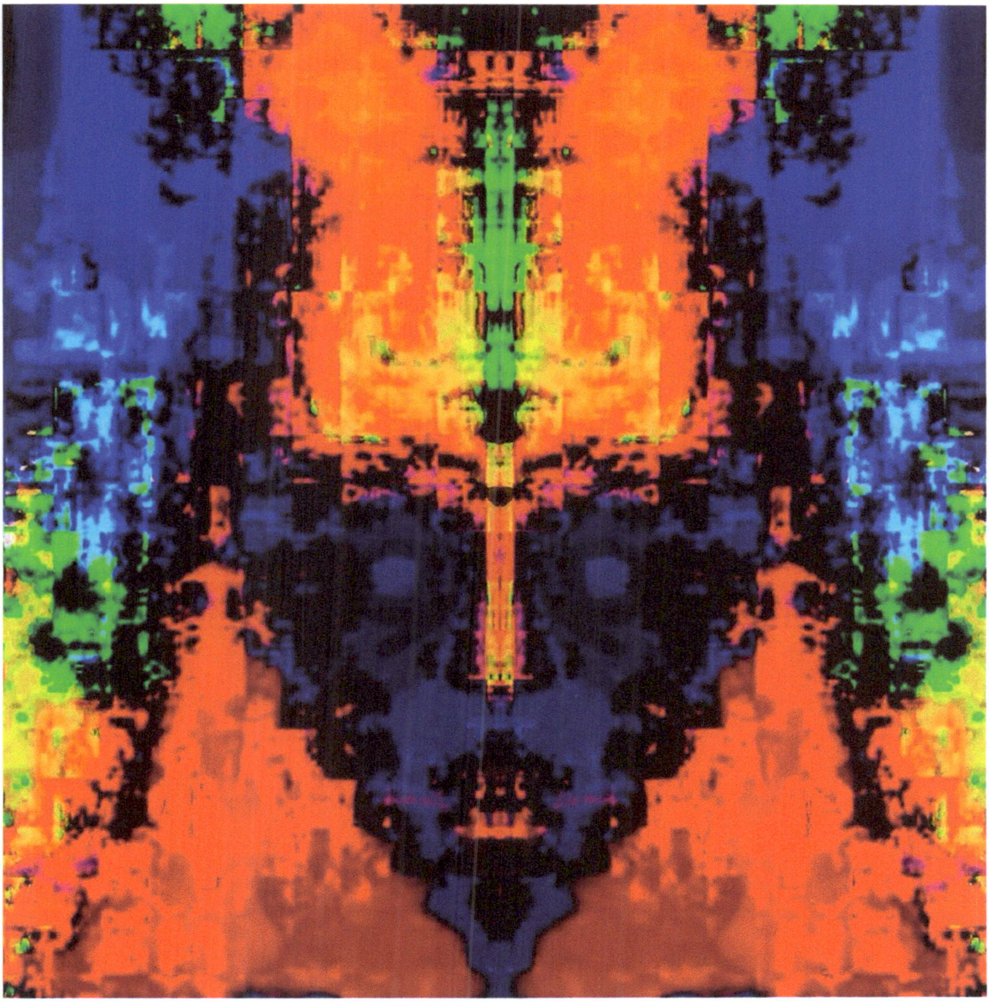

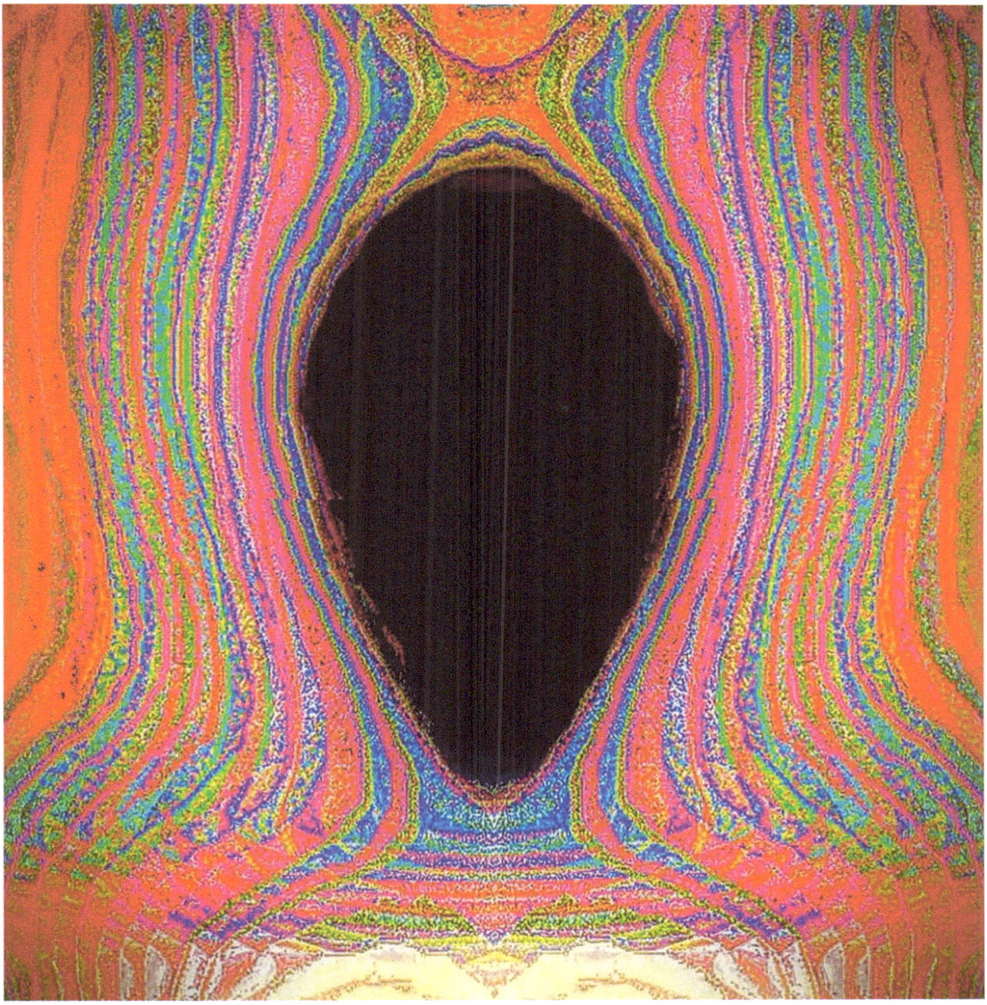

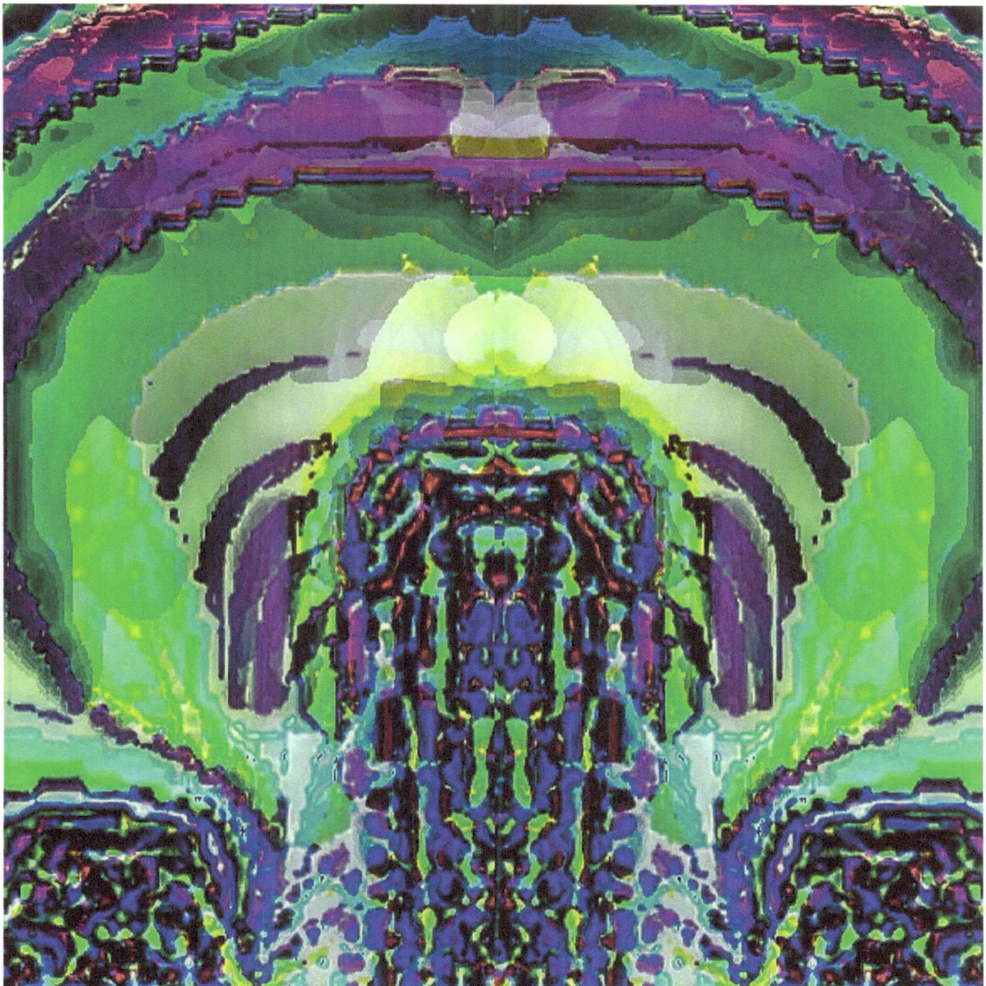

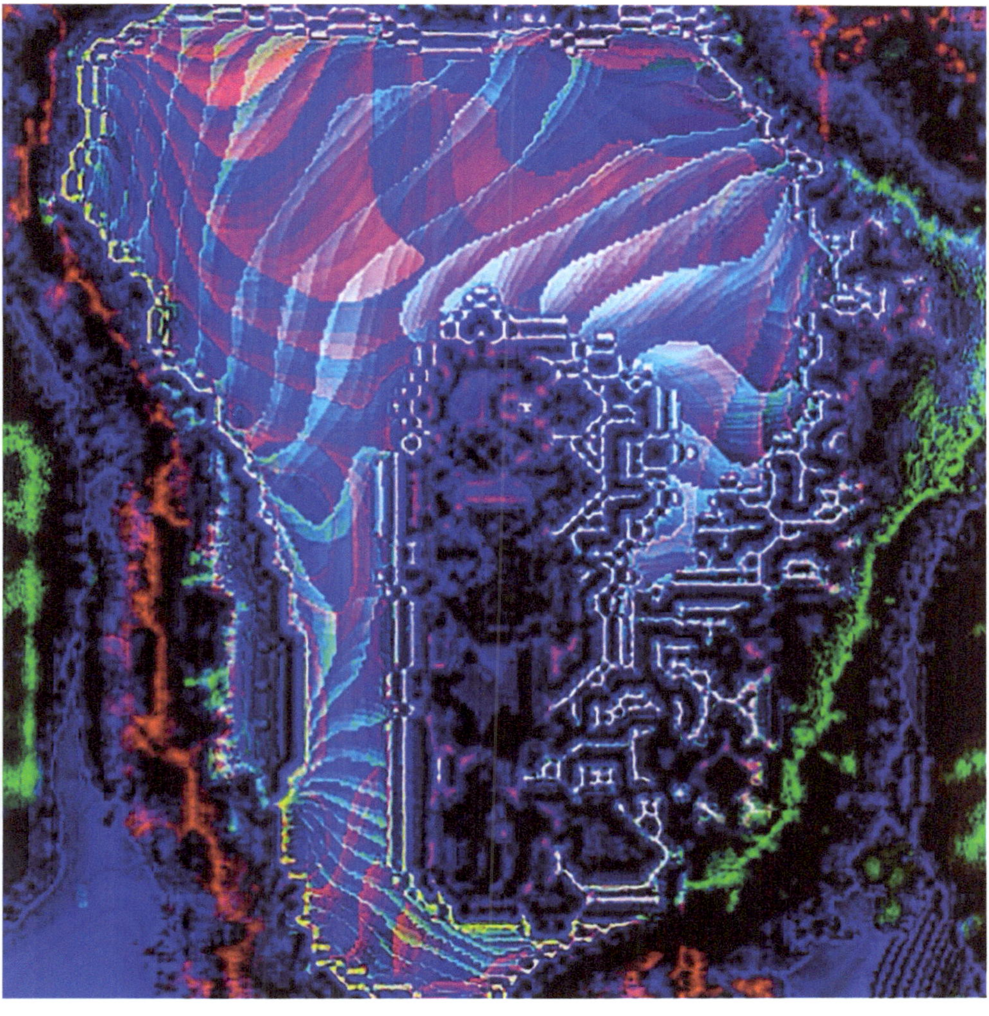

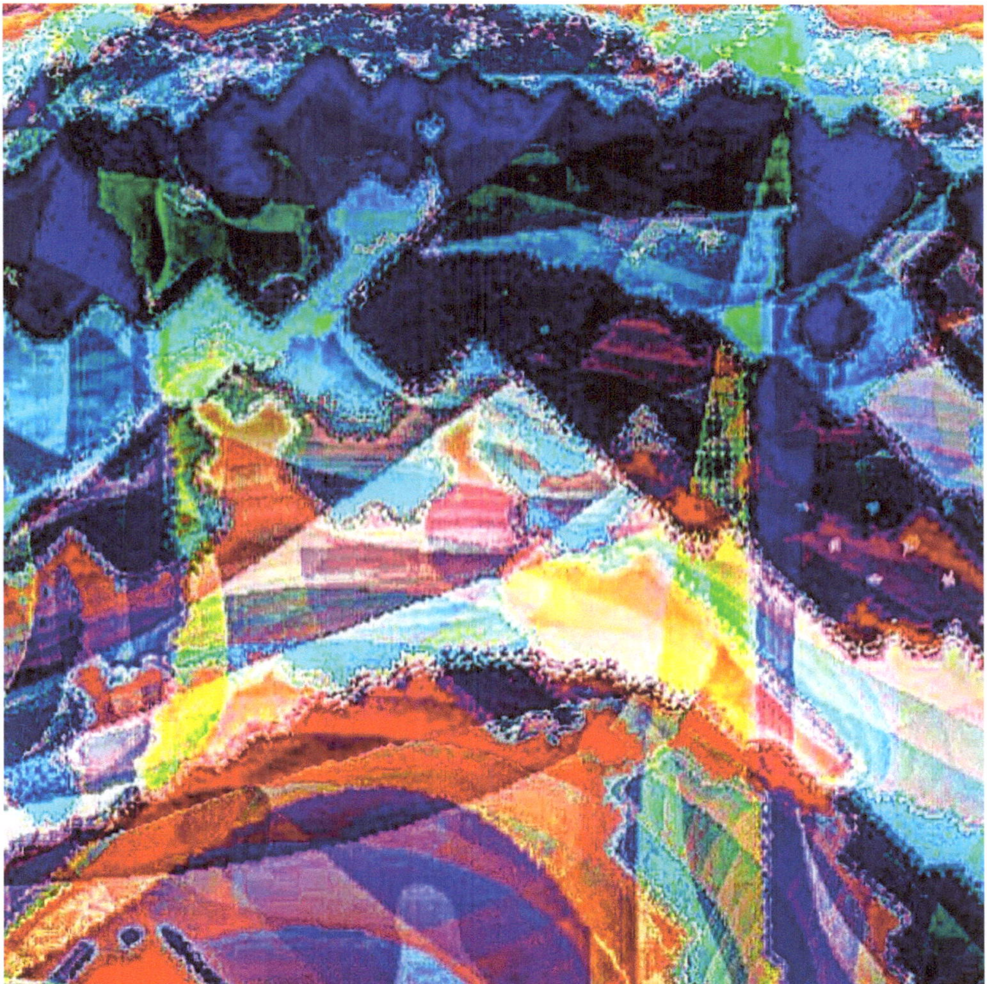

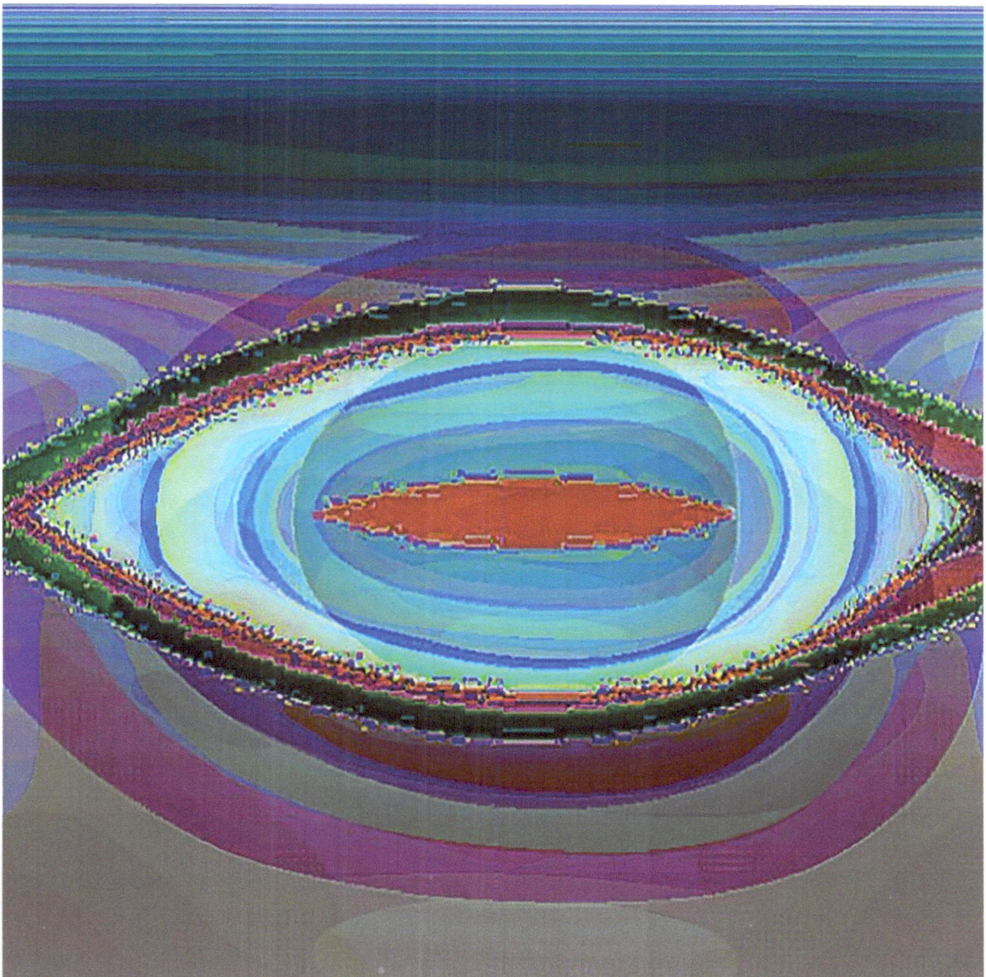

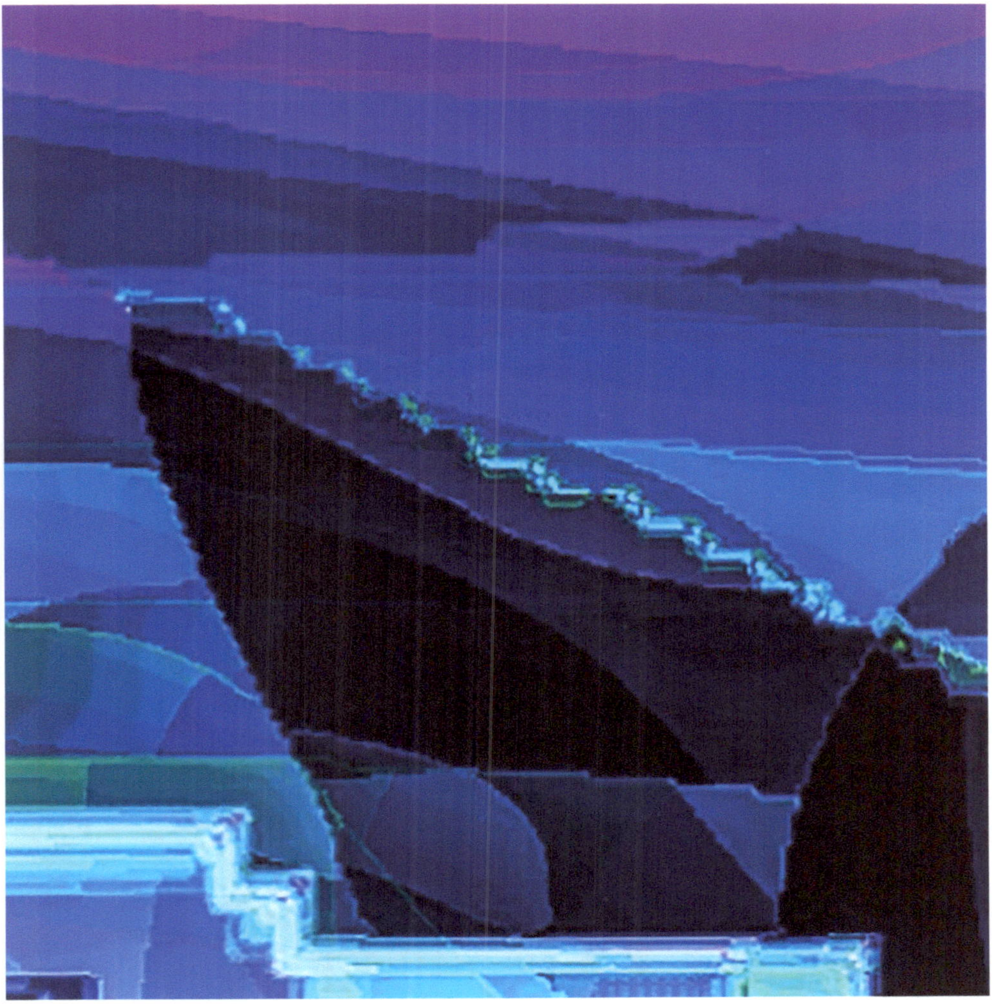

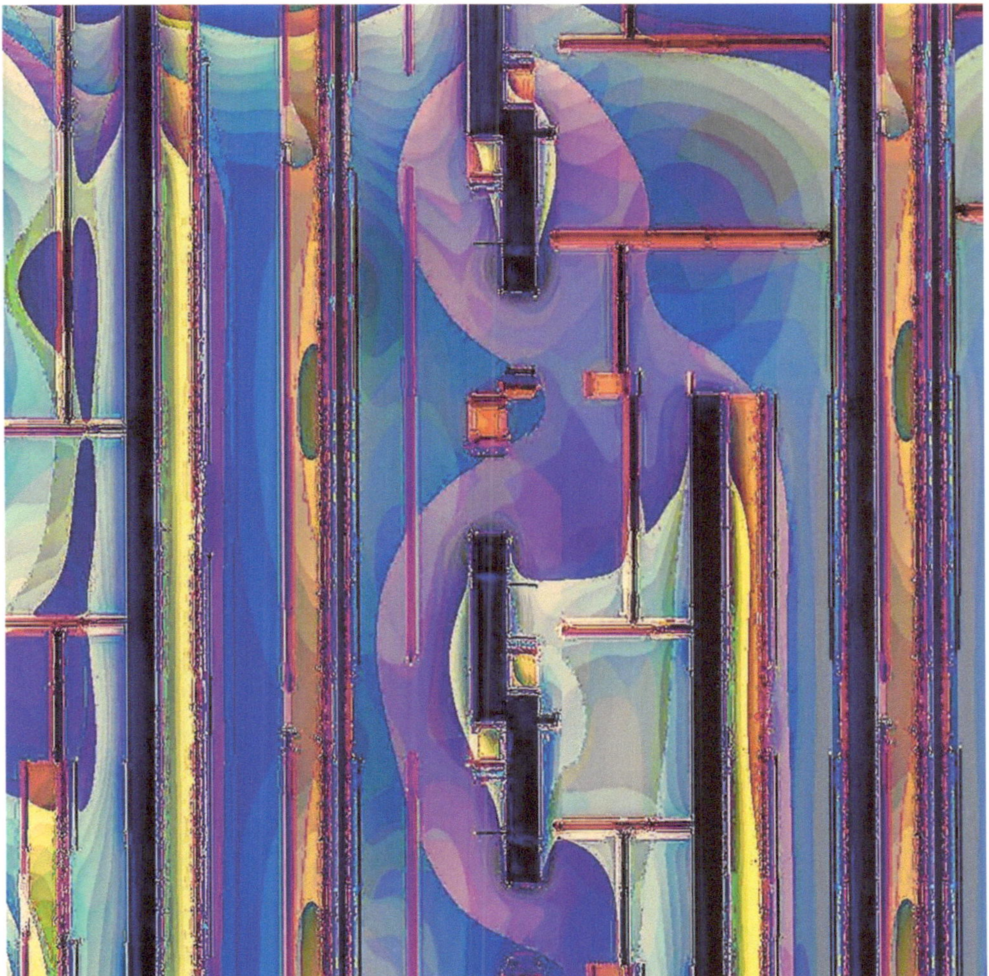

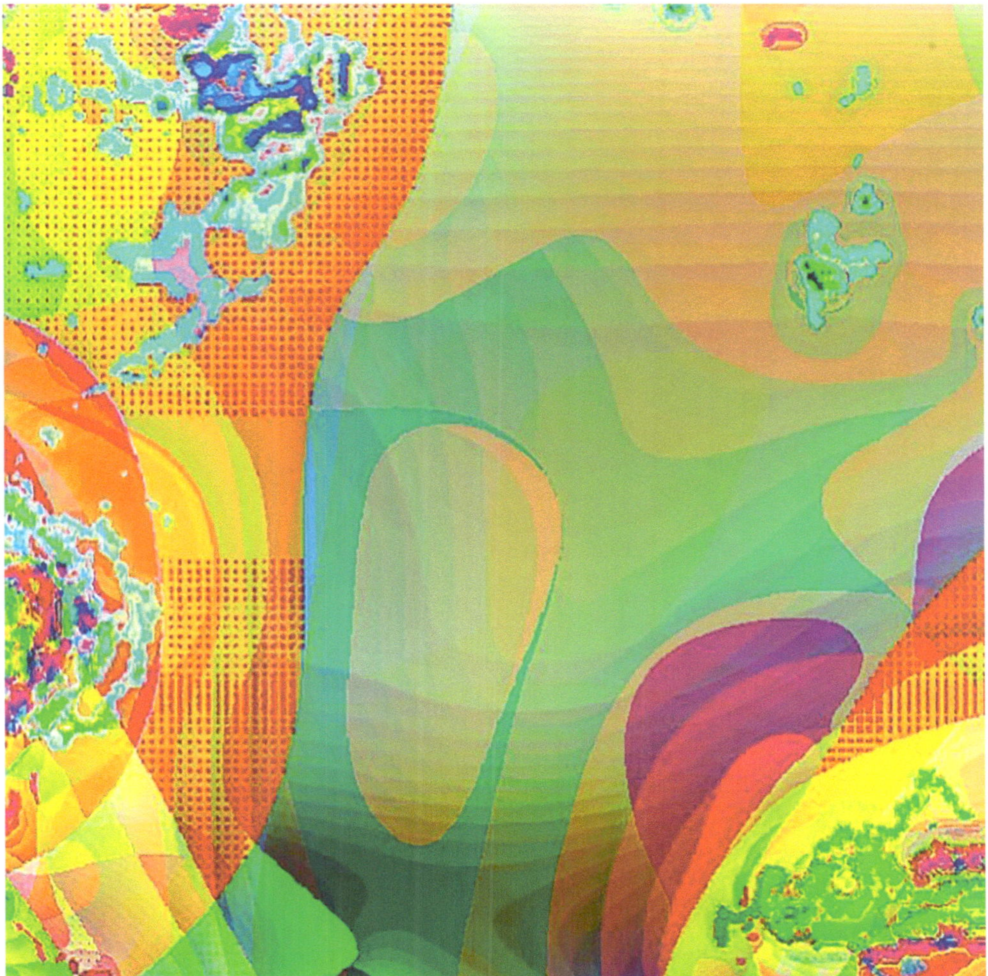

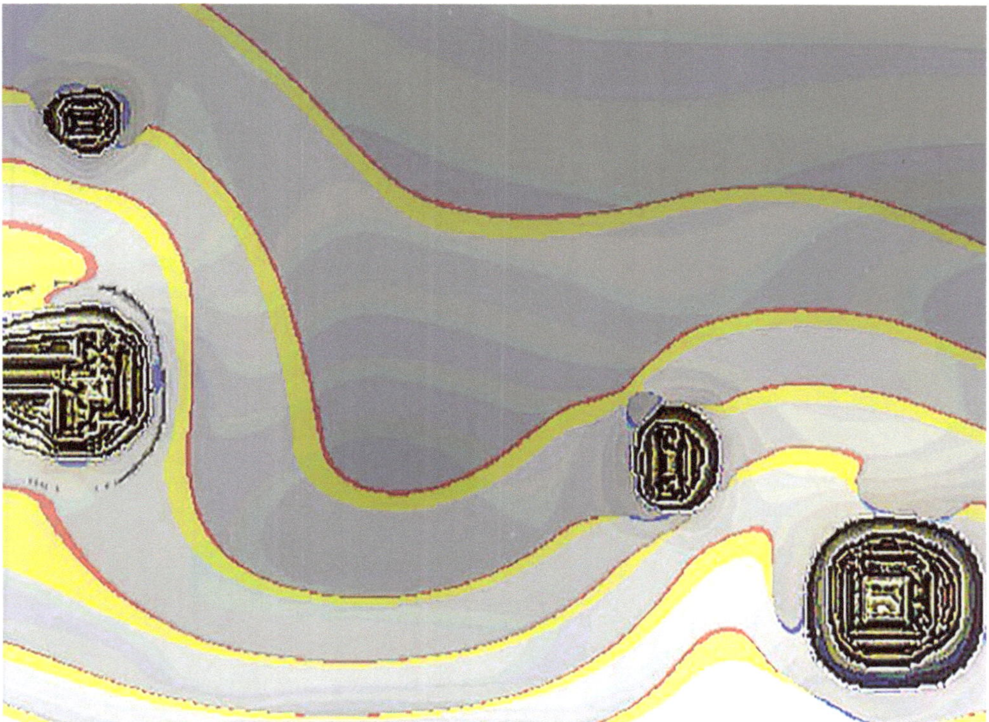

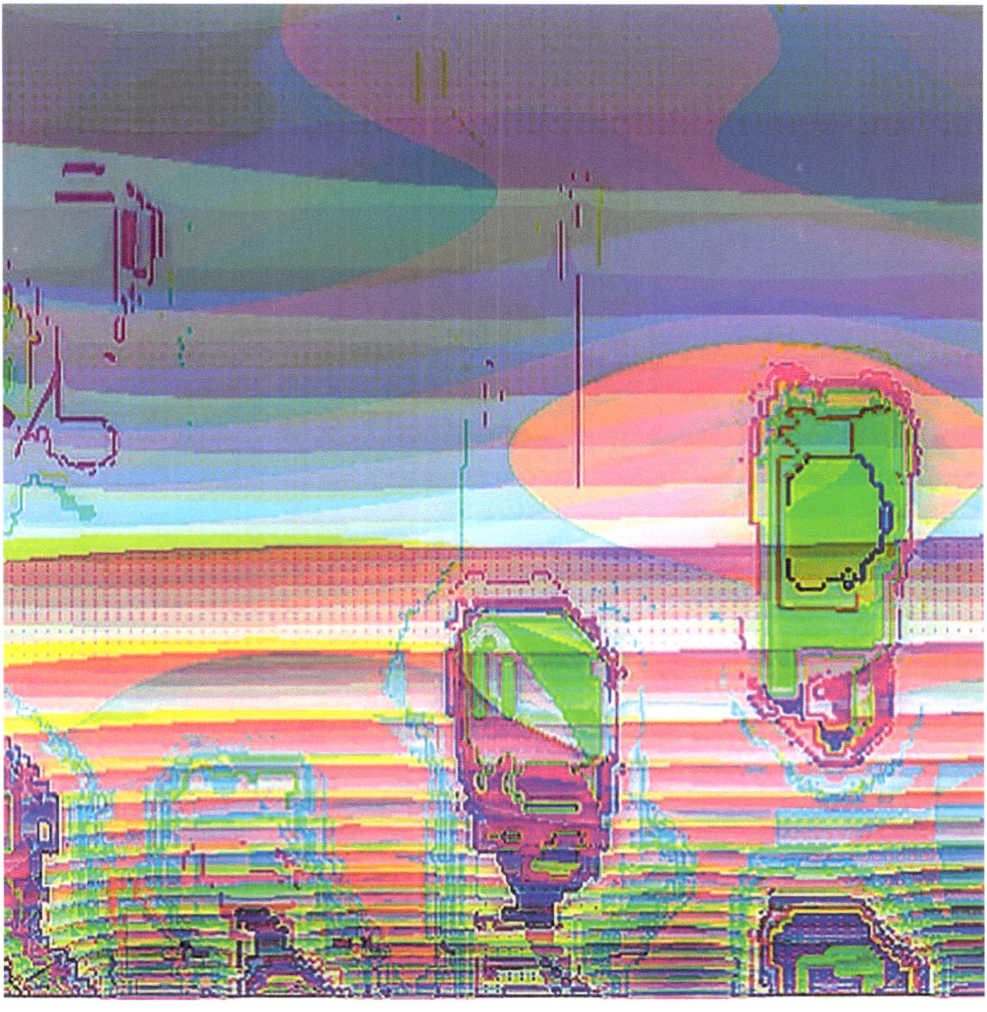

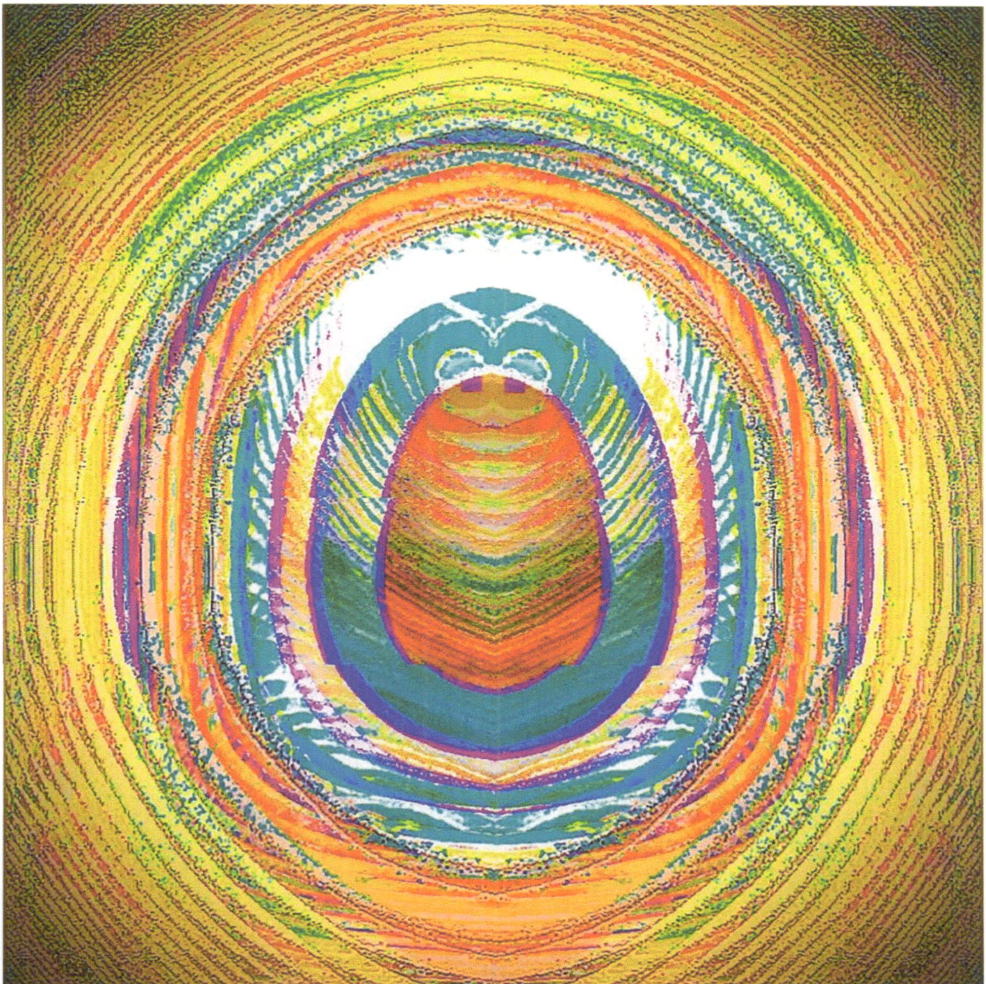

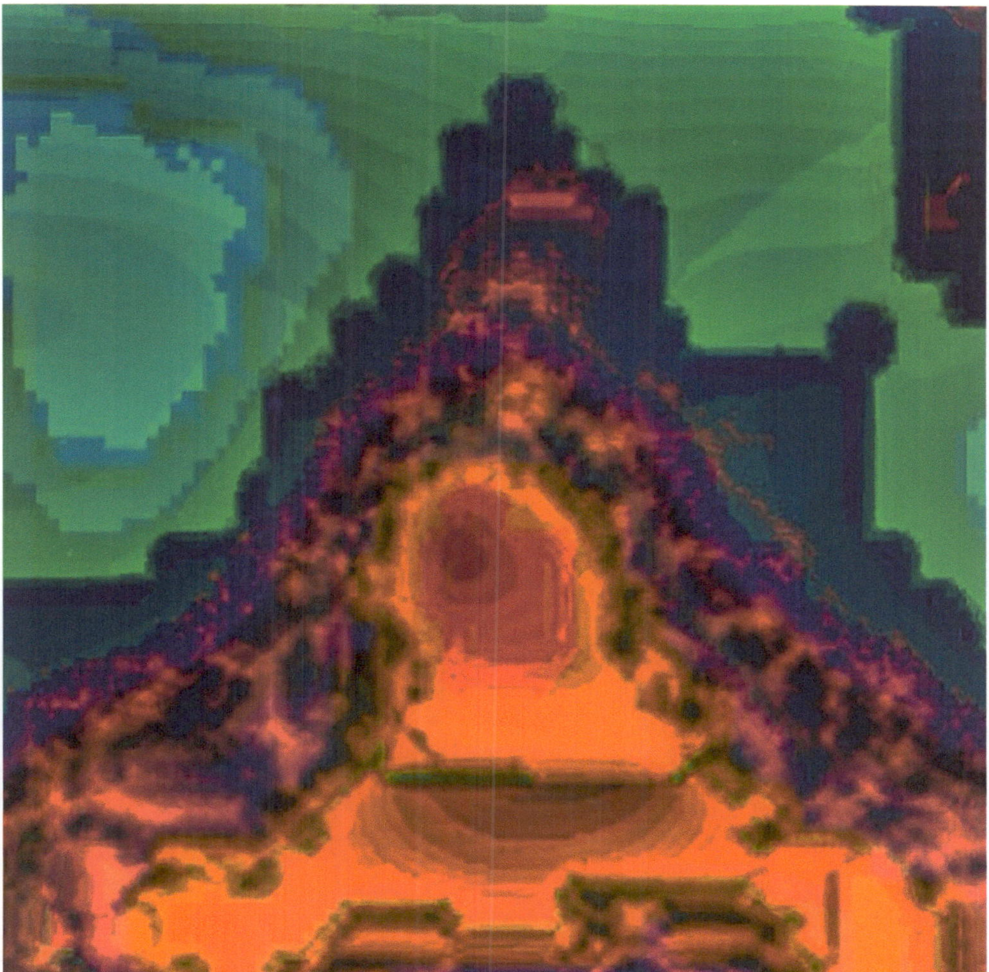

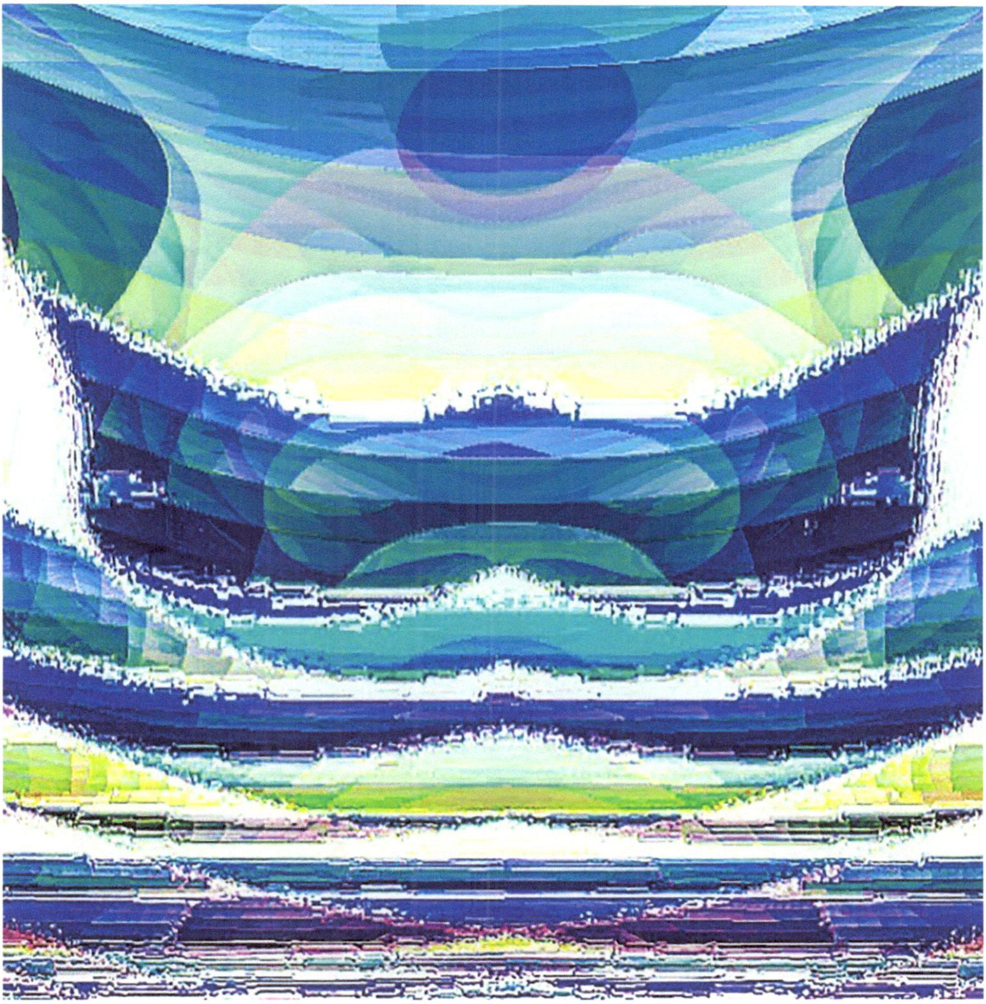

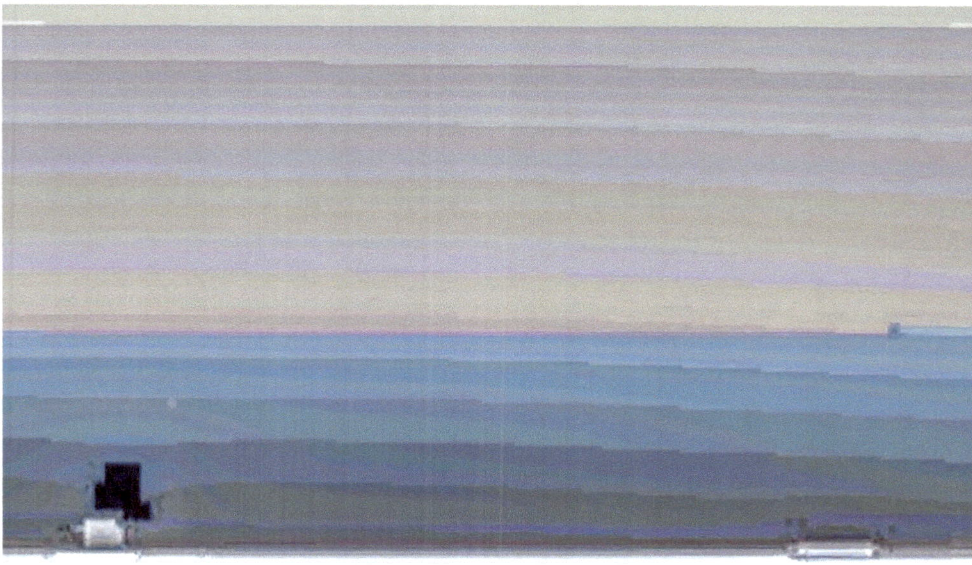

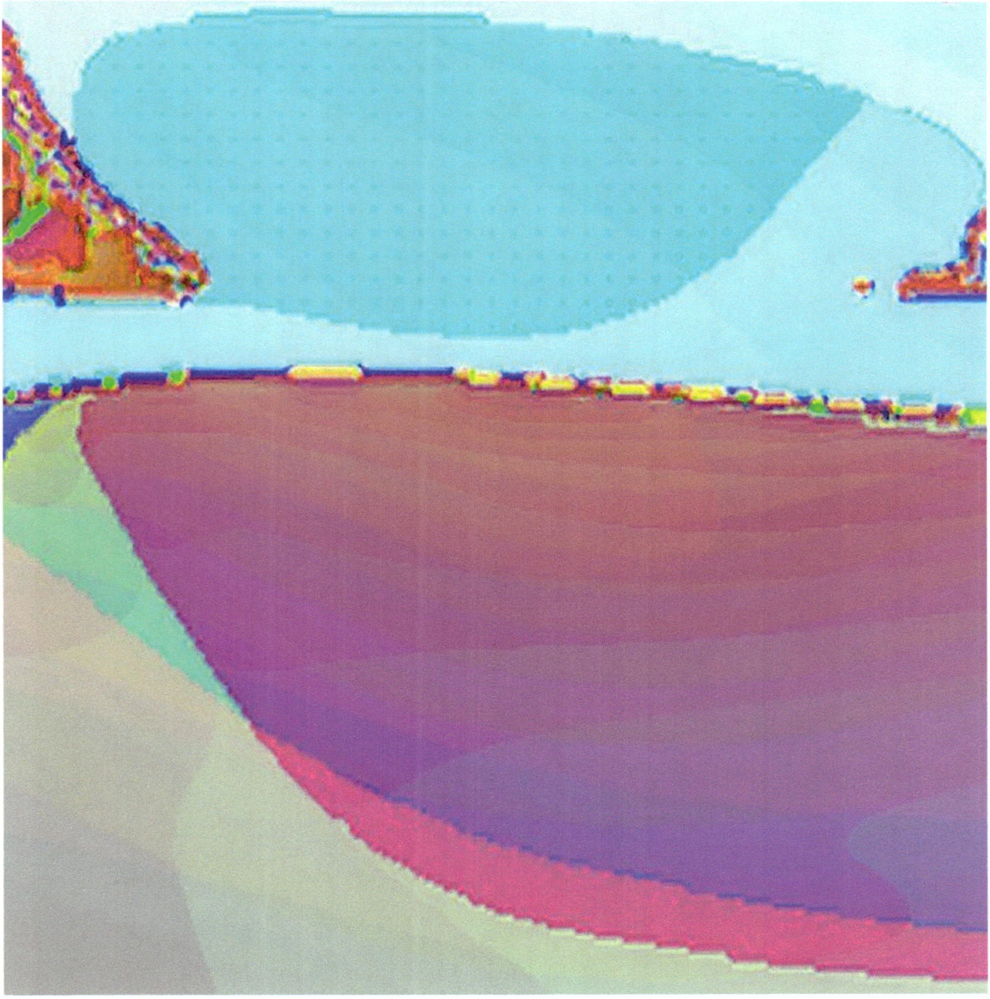

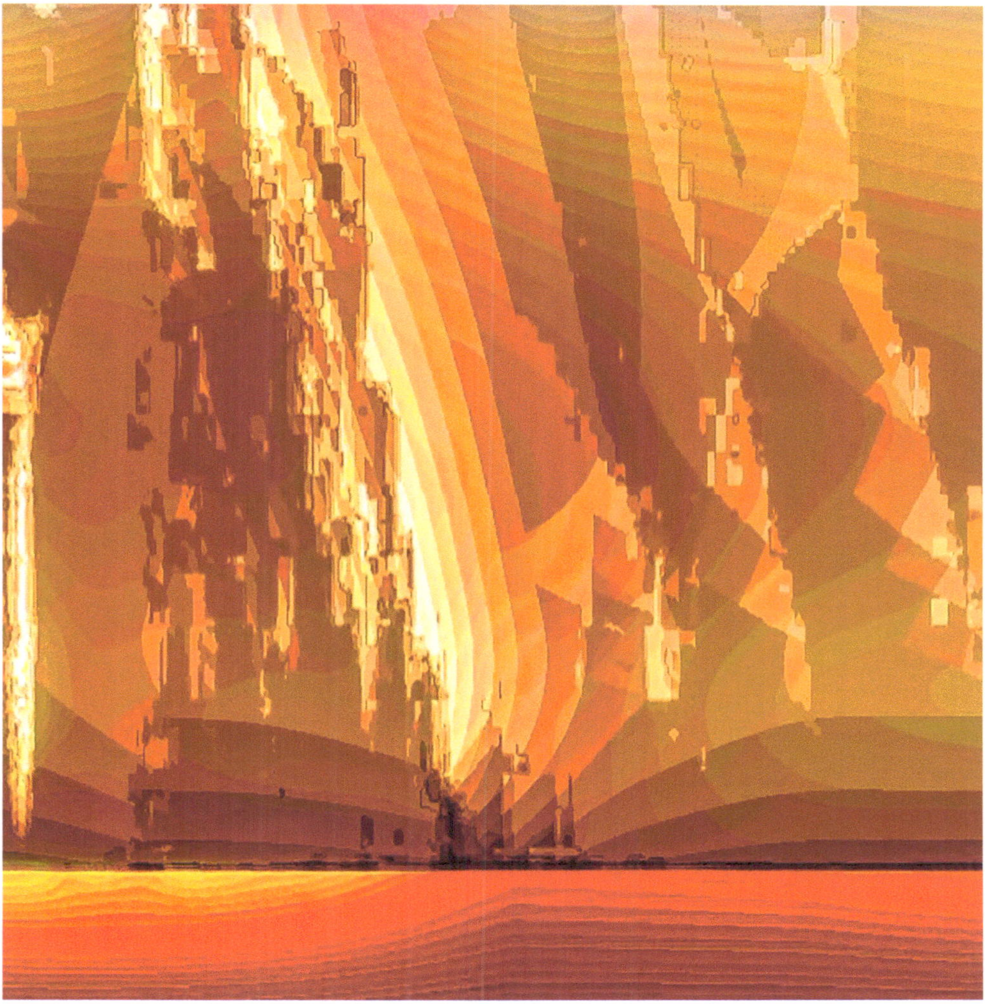

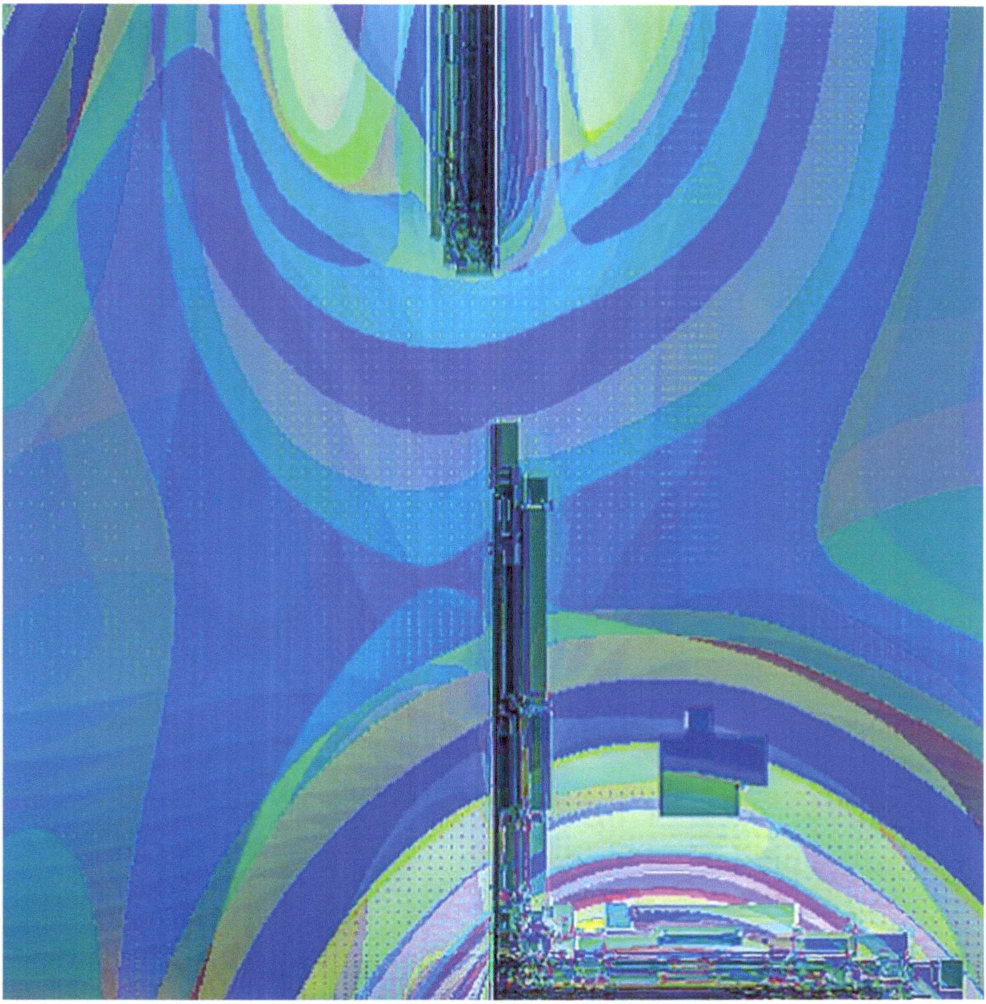

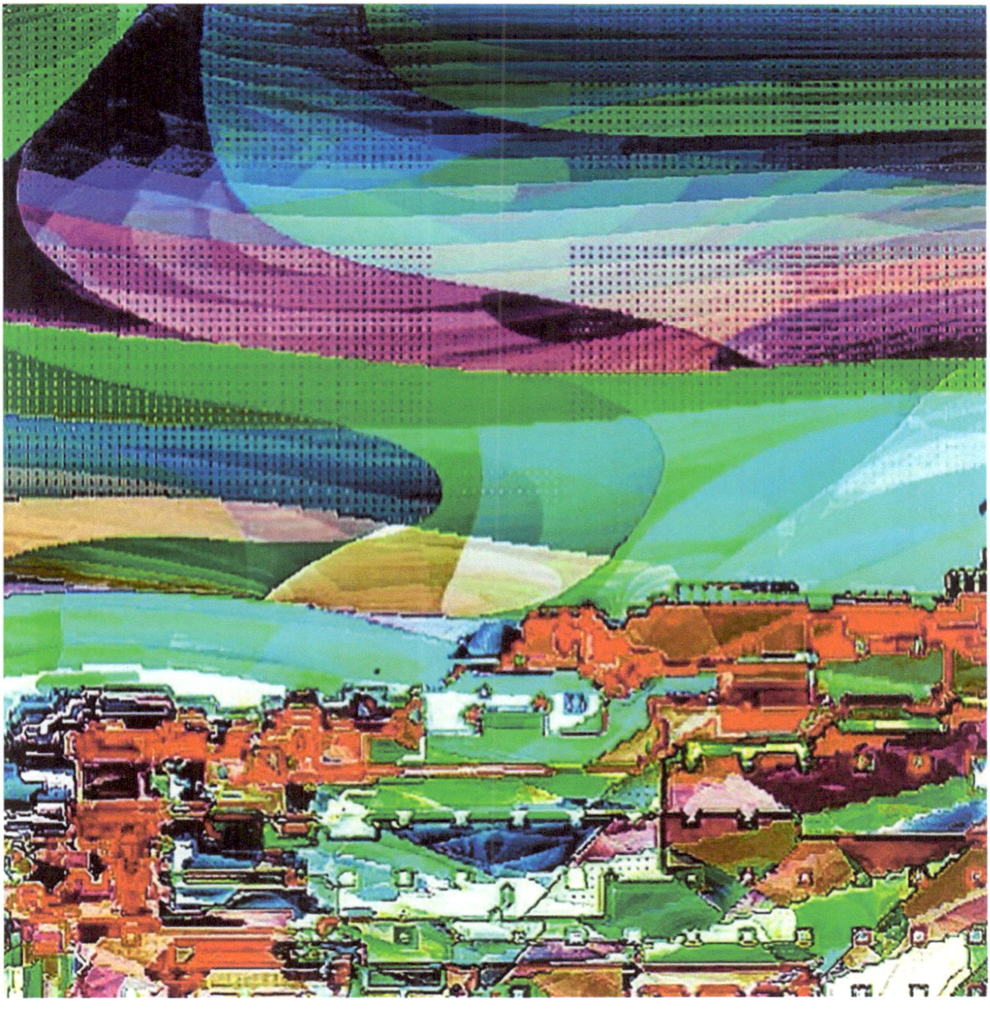

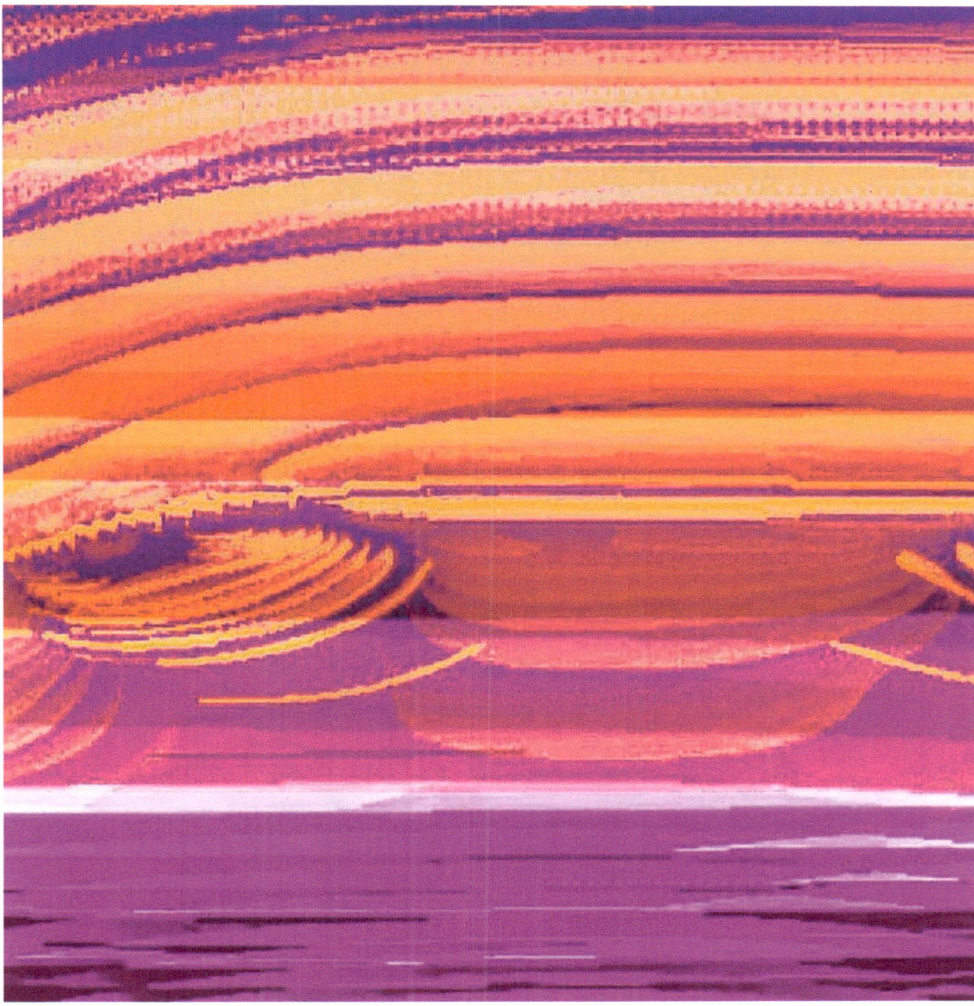

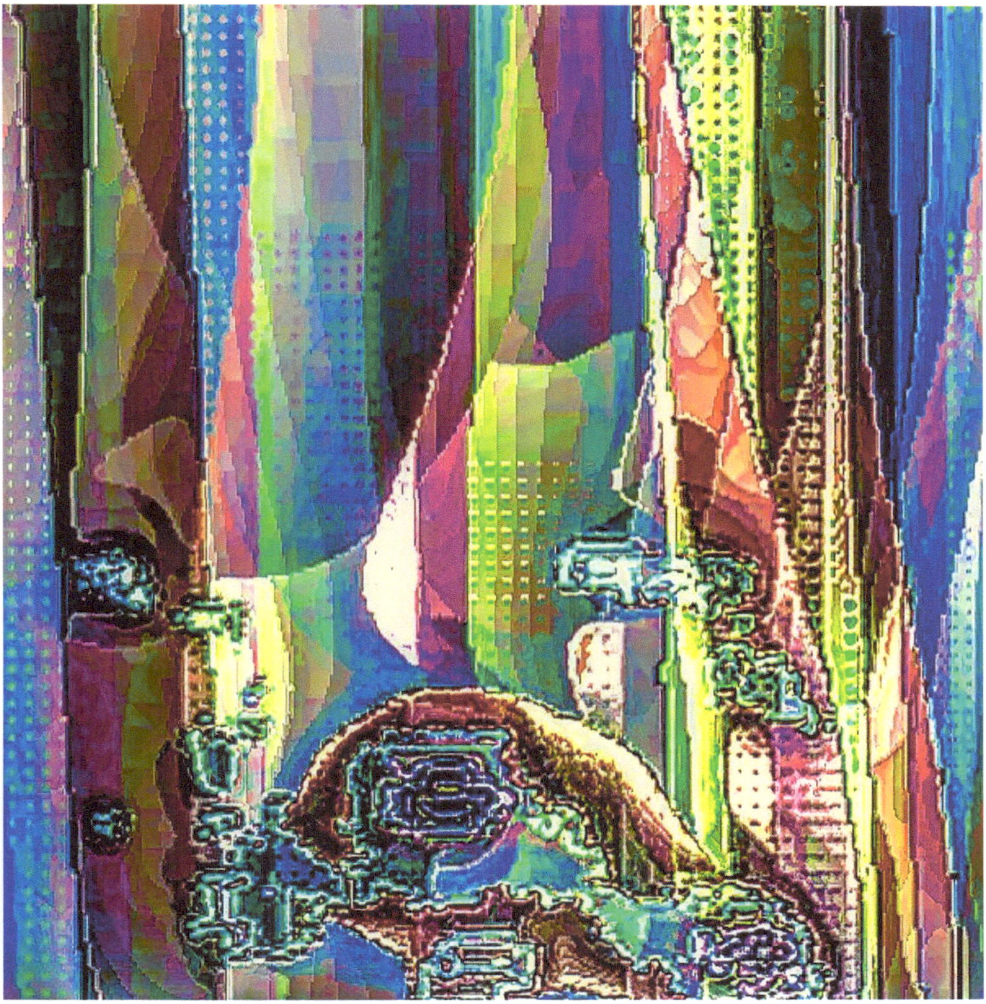

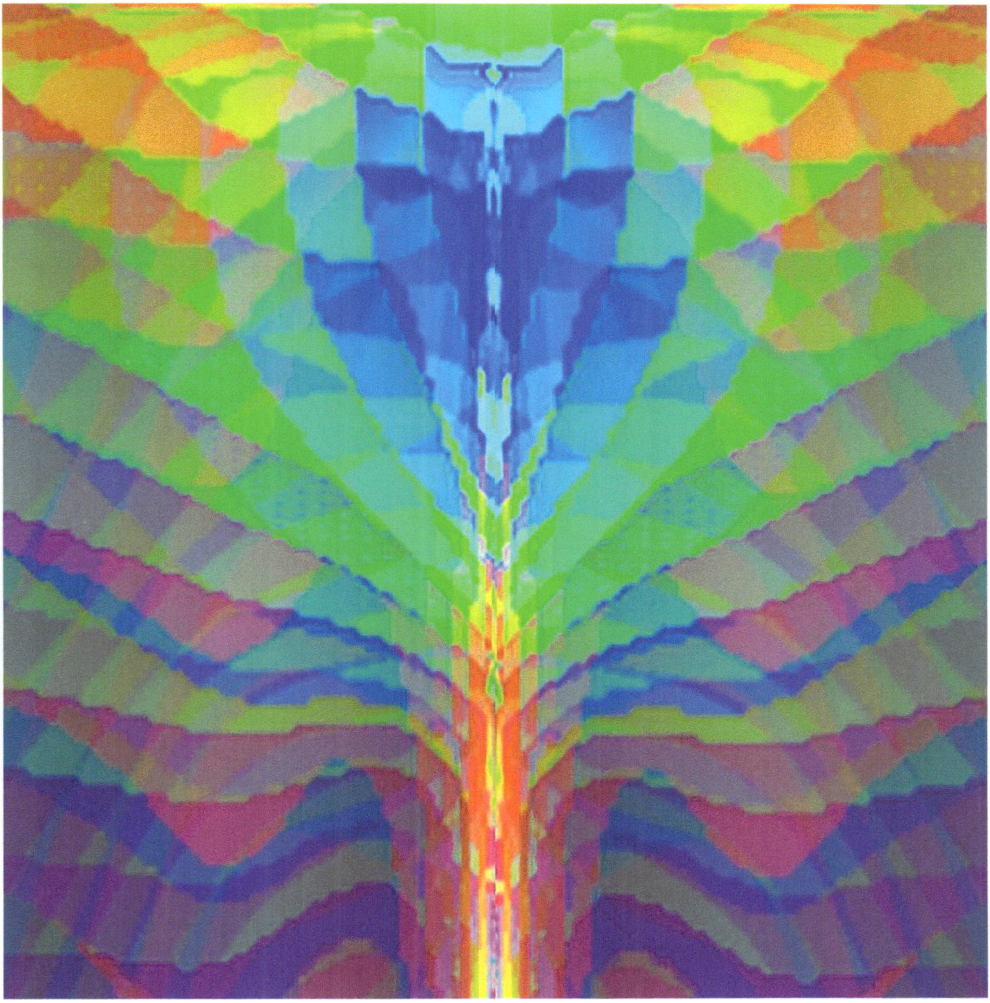

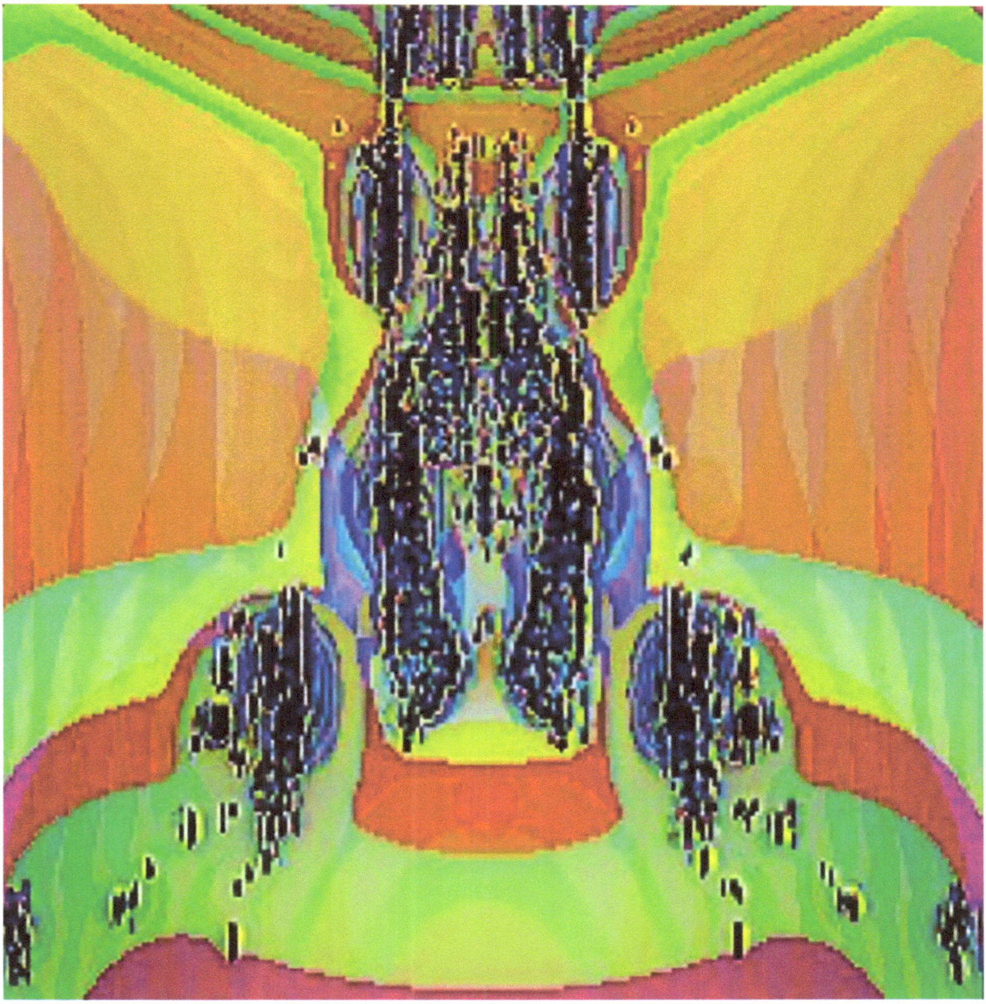

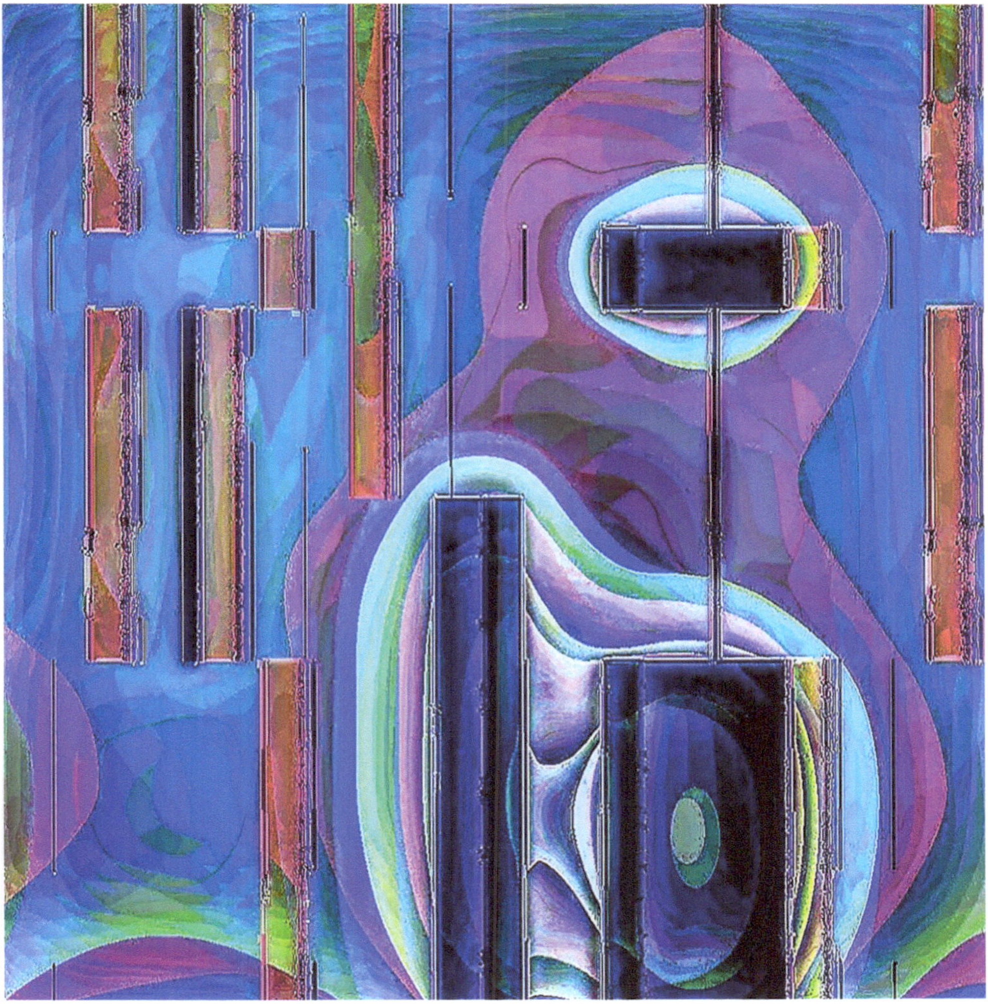

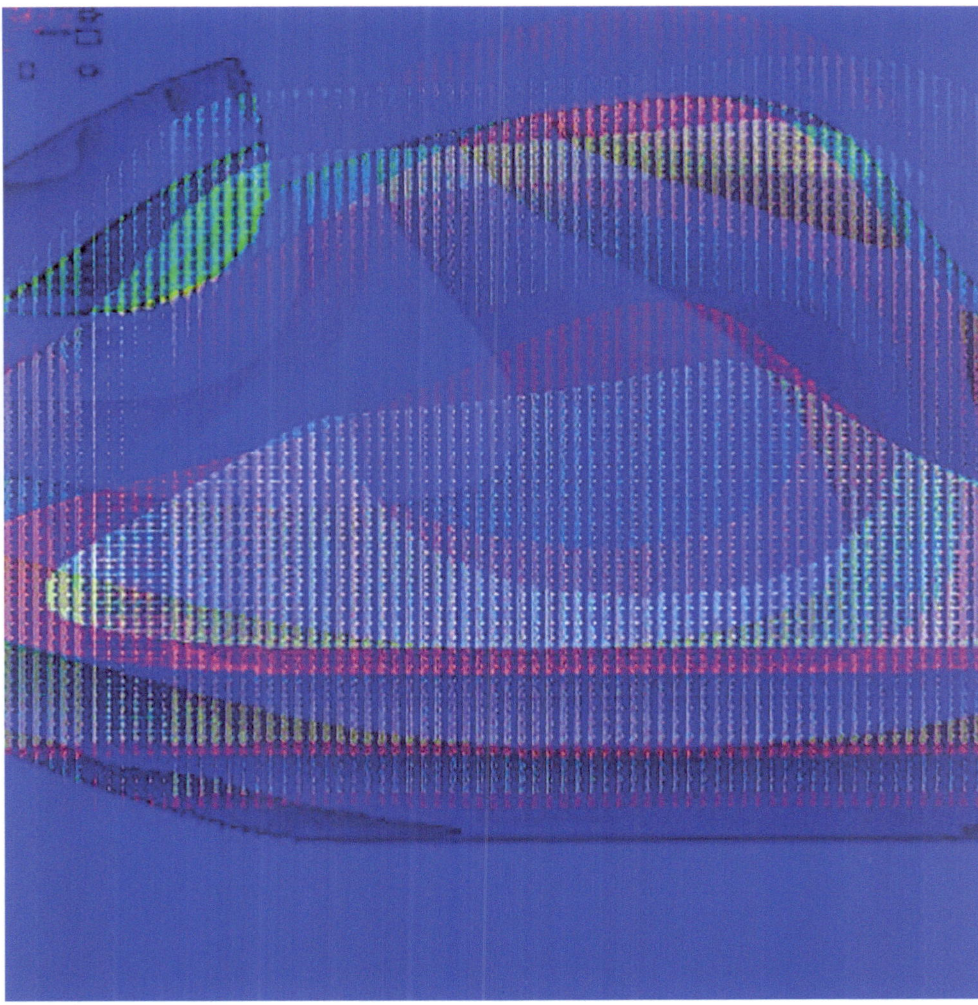

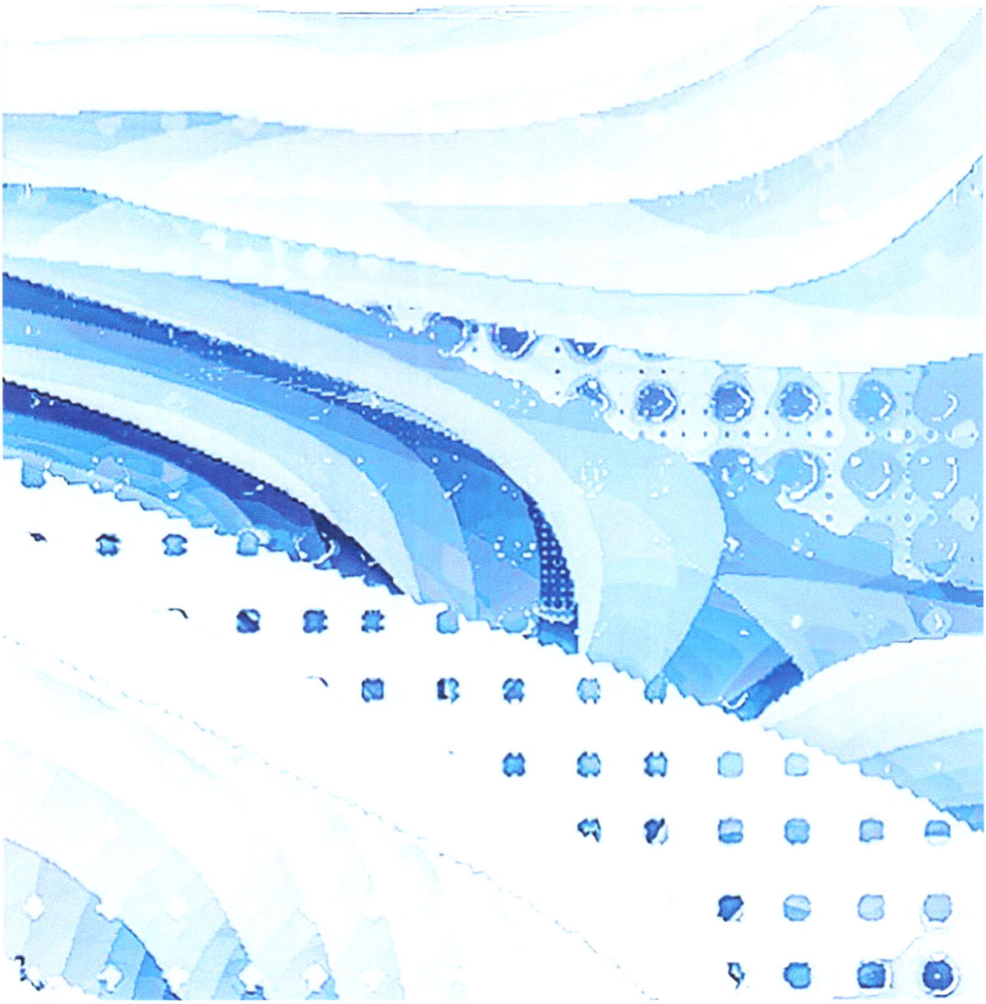

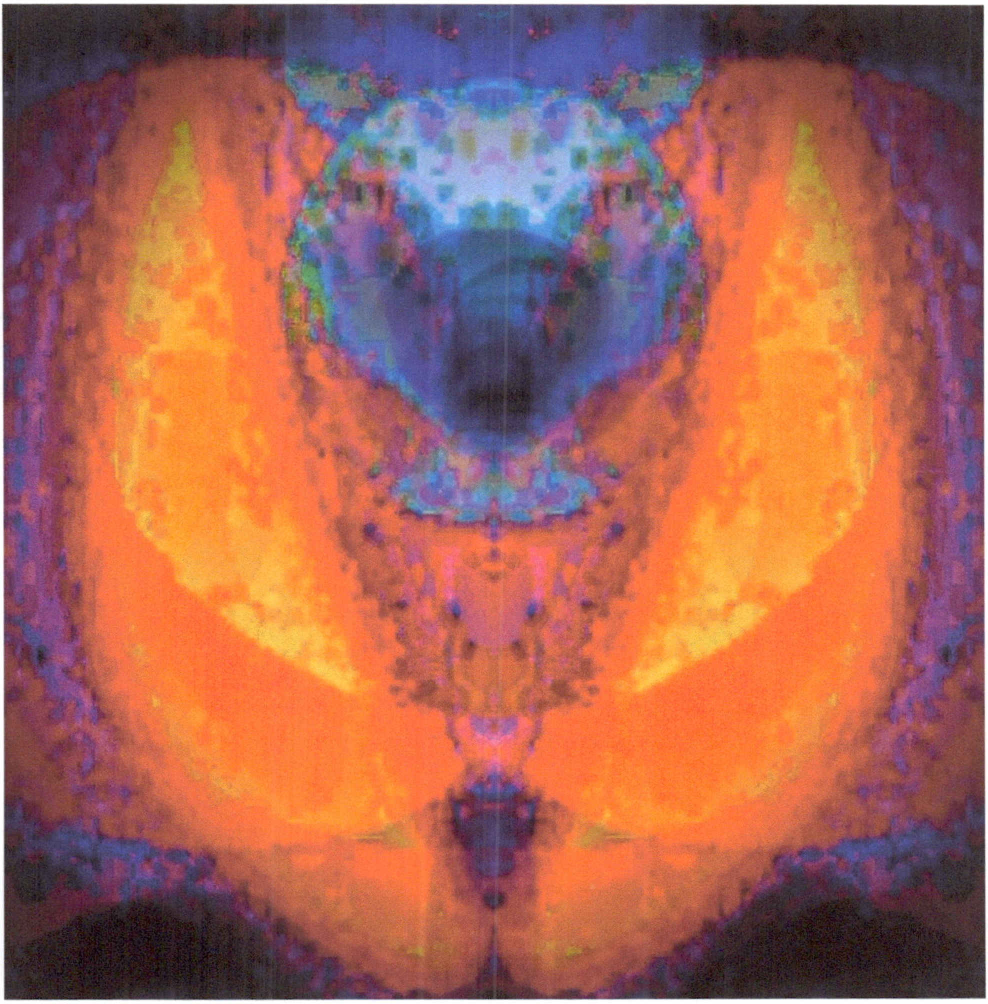

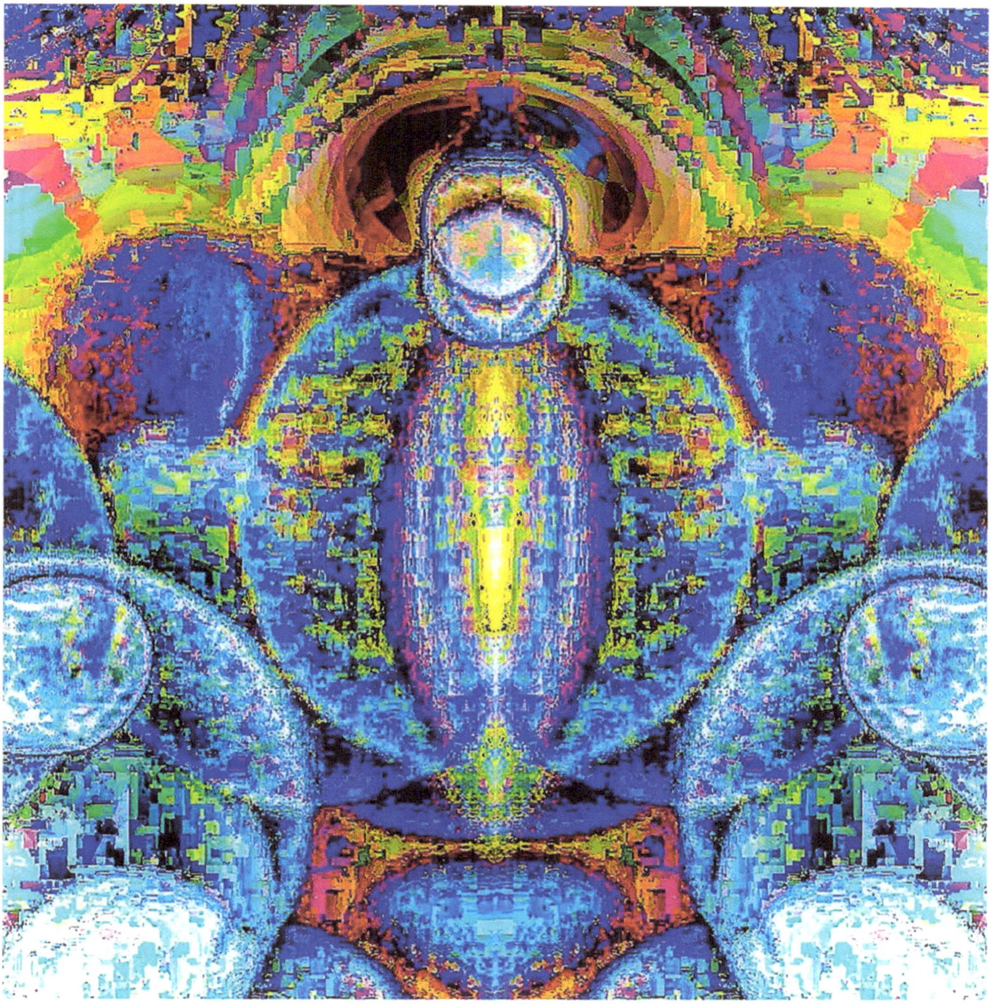

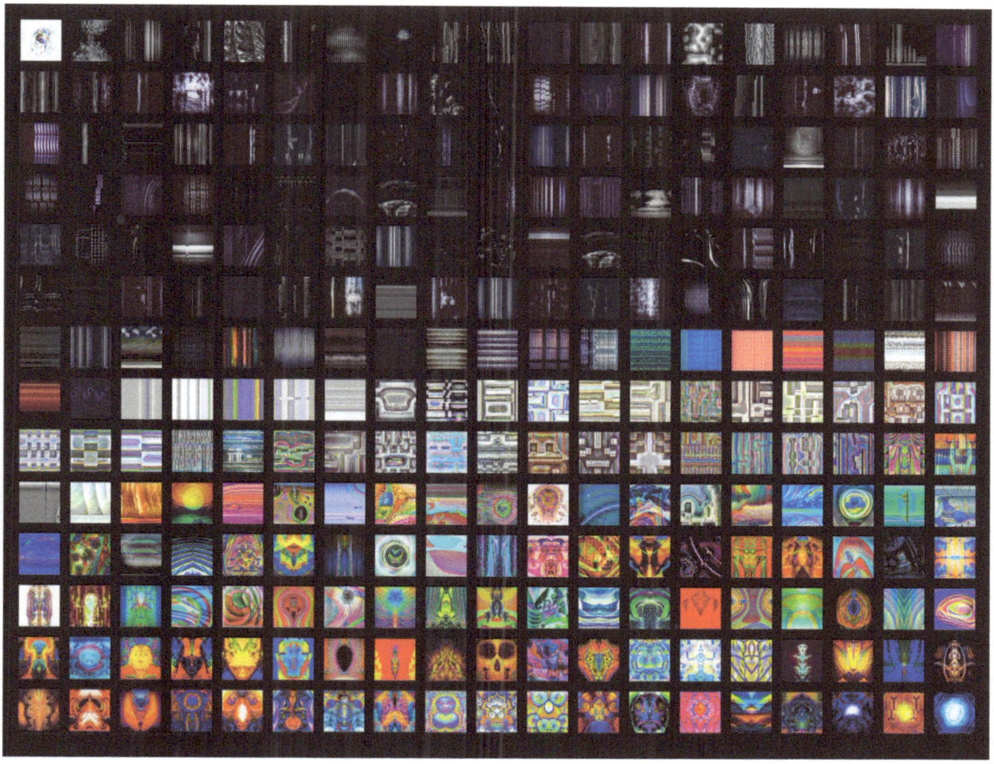

Instaglitch Compilation Poster
2021, full color, glossy 70lb stock
18x24 inches, edition of 25

contains 266 *Instaglitches*